50 Sugar Treat Recipes for Home

By: Kelly Johnson

Table of Contents

- Chocolate Chip Cookies
- Vanilla Cupcakes
- Fudge Brownies
- Lemon Bars
- Oatmeal Raisin Cookies
- Peanut Butter Cookies
- Red Velvet Cake
- Carrot Cake
- Banana Bread
- Apple Pie
- Chocolate Fudge
- Cheesecake
- Cinnamon Rolls
- Snickerdoodle Cookies
- Strawberry Shortcake
- Blueberry Muffins
- Key Lime Pie
- Tiramisu
- Pecan Pie
- Coconut Macaroons
- Gingerbread Cookies
- Raspberry Tart
- S'mores Bars
- Pumpkin Bread
- Almond Biscotti
- Pineapple Upside-Down Cake
- Chocolate Eclairs
- Coffee Cake
- Creme Brulee
- Rice Krispie Treats
- Meringue Cookies
- Orange Sorbet
- Peanut Brittle
- Fig Newtons
- Maple Pecan Bars
- Nutella Crepes

- Mint Chocolate Chip Ice Cream
- Amaretto Truffles
- Cranberry Pistachio Biscotti
- Mango Sorbet
- Black Forest Cake
- Panna Cotta
- Caramel Popcorn
- White Chocolate Blondies
- Lavender Shortbread
- Churros
- Peppermint Bark
- Apple Crisp
- Chocolate Covered Strawberries
- Lemon Meringue Pie

Chocolate Chip Cookies

Ingredients:

- 1 cup (2 sticks) unsalted butter, softened
- 3/4 cup granulated sugar
- 3/4 cup packed light brown sugar
- 1 teaspoon vanilla extract
- 2 large eggs
- 2 1/4 cups all-purpose flour
- 1 teaspoon baking soda
- 1/2 teaspoon salt
- 2 cups semisweet chocolate chips

Instructions:

1. Preheat your oven to 350°F (175°C). Line baking sheets with parchment paper or silicone baking mats.
2. In a large bowl, cream together the softened butter, granulated sugar, brown sugar, and vanilla extract until smooth and creamy.
3. Beat in the eggs one at a time until well combined.
4. In a separate bowl, whisk together the flour, baking soda, and salt.
5. Gradually add the dry ingredients to the wet ingredients, mixing until just combined.
6. Fold in the chocolate chips with a spatula or wooden spoon until evenly distributed throughout the dough.
7. Drop tablespoon-sized balls of dough onto the prepared baking sheets, spacing them about 2 inches apart.
8. Bake in the preheated oven for 9-11 minutes, or until the edges are golden brown. The centers may still look slightly underdone, but they will continue to set as they cool.
9. Allow the cookies to cool on the baking sheet for a few minutes before transferring them to a wire rack to cool completely.
10. Enjoy your homemade chocolate chip cookies with a glass of milk or your favorite beverage!

This recipe makes about 3 dozen cookies, depending on the size of your dough balls. Adjust baking time slightly for softer or crispier cookies according to your preference.

Vanilla Cupcakes

Ingredients:

- 1 1/2 cups all-purpose flour
- 1 1/2 teaspoons baking powder
- 1/4 teaspoon salt
- 1/2 cup unsalted butter, softened
- 1 cup granulated sugar
- 2 large eggs, at room temperature
- 2 teaspoons vanilla extract
- 1/2 cup milk, at room temperature

Instructions:

1. Preheat your oven to 350°F (175°C). Line a muffin tin with cupcake liners.
2. In a medium bowl, whisk together the flour, baking powder, and salt. Set aside.
3. In a large bowl, cream together the softened butter and granulated sugar until light and fluffy, using a hand mixer or stand mixer.
4. Add the eggs one at a time, mixing well after each addition. Mix in the vanilla extract.
5. Gradually add the dry ingredients to the wet ingredients, alternating with the milk, beginning and ending with the dry ingredients. Mix until just combined; do not overmix.
6. Fill each cupcake liner about 2/3 full with batter.
7. Bake for 18-20 minutes, or until a toothpick inserted into the center comes out clean.
8. Remove from the oven and allow the cupcakes to cool in the pan for 5 minutes, then transfer them to a wire rack to cool completely before frosting.

Vanilla Buttercream Frosting:

- 1 cup unsalted butter, softened
- 4 cups powdered sugar, sifted
- 1 teaspoon vanilla extract
- 2-3 tablespoons heavy cream or milk

Instructions for Frosting:

1. In a large bowl, beat the softened butter until creamy and smooth.
2. Gradually add the powdered sugar, one cup at a time, beating well after each addition.
3. Mix in the vanilla extract.
4. Add the heavy cream or milk, 1 tablespoon at a time, until the frosting reaches your desired consistency.
5. Beat on medium-high speed for about 3-4 minutes until the frosting is light and fluffy.
6. Once the cupcakes are completely cool, frost them using a piping bag fitted with your favorite piping tip, or simply spread the frosting with a knife.
7. Optionally, decorate with sprinkles, chocolate shavings, or any other toppings of your choice.

Enjoy these classic vanilla cupcakes, perfect for any occasion!

Fudge Brownies

Ingredients:

- 1 cup (2 sticks) unsalted butter
- 2 cups granulated sugar
- 4 large eggs
- 1 teaspoon vanilla extract
- 1 cup all-purpose flour
- 3/4 cup unsweetened cocoa powder
- 1/2 teaspoon salt
- 1 cup semisweet chocolate chips (optional)

Instructions:

1. Preheat your oven to 350°F (175°C). Grease a 9x13 inch baking pan or line it with parchment paper.
2. In a medium saucepan, melt the butter over medium heat. Stir in the granulated sugar until well combined. Remove from heat and let it cool slightly.
3. In a large bowl, whisk together the eggs and vanilla extract.
4. Gradually pour the slightly cooled butter-sugar mixture into the egg mixture, whisking constantly until smooth.
5. In another bowl, sift together the flour, cocoa powder, and salt.
6. Gradually add the dry ingredients to the wet ingredients, stirring with a rubber spatula or wooden spoon until just combined. Do not overmix.
7. If using, fold in the chocolate chips until evenly distributed in the batter.
8. Pour the batter into the prepared baking pan and spread it out evenly with a spatula.
9. Bake in the preheated oven for 25-30 minutes, or until a toothpick inserted into the center comes out with a few moist crumbs. Be careful not to overbake if you prefer fudgy brownies.
10. Remove from the oven and let the brownies cool completely in the pan on a wire rack before cutting into squares.
11. Enjoy your rich and fudgy homemade brownies!

Lemon Bars

Ingredients:

For the crust:

- 1 cup (2 sticks) unsalted butter, softened
- 1/2 cup granulated sugar
- 2 cups all-purpose flour
- 1/4 teaspoon salt

For the lemon filling:

- 1 1/2 cups granulated sugar
- 1/4 cup all-purpose flour
- 4 large eggs
- 2/3 cup freshly squeezed lemon juice (about 4-5 lemons)
- Zest of 1 lemon
- Powdered sugar, for dusting

Instructions:

1. **Preheat** your oven to 350°F (175°C). Grease a 9x13 inch baking pan or line it with parchment paper, leaving an overhang for easy removal.
2. **Make the crust:**
    - In a large bowl, cream together the softened butter and granulated sugar until light and fluffy.
    - Gradually add the flour and salt, mixing until well combined and a crumbly dough forms.
    - Press the dough evenly into the bottom of the prepared baking pan.
3. **Bake the crust** in the preheated oven for 20-25 minutes, or until lightly golden brown around the edges. Remove from the oven and let it cool slightly.
4. **Make the lemon filling:**
    - In a separate bowl, whisk together the granulated sugar and flour.
    - Whisk in the eggs until smooth and well combined.
    - Stir in the freshly squeezed lemon juice and lemon zest until the mixture is smooth and slightly thickened.
5. **Pour the lemon filling** over the baked crust, spreading it out evenly with a spatula.
6. **Bake** for an additional 20-25 minutes, or until the filling is set and the edges are lightly golden brown.
7. **Remove** from the oven and let the lemon bars cool completely in the pan on a wire rack.
8. **Once cooled**, dust with powdered sugar.
9. **Chill** the lemon bars in the refrigerator for at least 1-2 hours before slicing into squares.
10. **Serve** and enjoy these tangy, sweet, and refreshing lemon bars!

These lemon bars are perfect for any occasion and are sure to be a hit with lemon lovers!

Oatmeal Raisin Cookies

Ingredients:

- 1 cup (2 sticks) unsalted butter, softened
- 1 cup packed light brown sugar
- 1/2 cup granulated sugar
- 2 large eggs
- 1 teaspoon vanilla extract
- 1 1/2 cups all-purpose flour
- 1 teaspoon baking soda
- 1 teaspoon ground cinnamon
- 1/2 teaspoon salt
- 3 cups old-fashioned rolled oats
- 1 cup raisins (or substitute with dried cranberries or chocolate chips)

Instructions:

1. **Preheat** your oven to 350°F (175°C). Line baking sheets with parchment paper or silicone baking mats.
2. **In a large bowl**, cream together the softened butter, brown sugar, and granulated sugar until light and fluffy.
3. **Add the eggs** one at a time, beating well after each addition. Stir in the vanilla extract.
4. **In a separate bowl**, whisk together the flour, baking soda, cinnamon, and salt.
5. **Gradually add** the dry ingredients to the wet ingredients, mixing until just combined.
6. **Fold in** the rolled oats and raisins (or other add-ins) until evenly distributed in the dough.
7. **Drop tablespoon-sized balls** of dough onto the prepared baking sheets, spacing them about 2 inches apart.
8. **Bake** in the preheated oven for 10-12 minutes, or until the edges are golden brown and the centers are set.
9. **Remove** from the oven and let the cookies cool on the baking sheet for a few minutes before transferring them to a wire rack to cool completely.
10. **Enjoy** your homemade oatmeal raisin cookies with a glass of milk or your favorite beverage!

These cookies are chewy, hearty, and perfect for snacking or sharing with friends and family.

Peanut Butter Cookies

Ingredients:

- 1 cup (2 sticks) unsalted butter, softened
- 1 cup creamy peanut butter
- 1 cup granulated sugar, plus extra for rolling
- 1 cup packed light brown sugar
- 2 large eggs
- 1 teaspoon vanilla extract
- 2 1/2 cups all-purpose flour
- 1 teaspoon baking powder
- 1/2 teaspoon baking soda
- 1/2 teaspoon salt

Instructions:

1. **Preheat** your oven to 350°F (175°C). Line baking sheets with parchment paper or silicone baking mats.
2. **In a large bowl**, cream together the softened butter, peanut butter, granulated sugar, and brown sugar until smooth and fluffy.
3. **Add the eggs** one at a time, mixing well after each addition. Stir in the vanilla extract.
4. **In a separate bowl**, whisk together the flour, baking powder, baking soda, and salt.
5. **Gradually add** the dry ingredients to the wet ingredients, mixing until just combined.
6. **Shape the dough** into tablespoon-sized balls. Roll each ball in granulated sugar to coat evenly.
7. **Place the balls** onto the prepared baking sheets, spacing them about 2 inches apart.
8. **Using a fork**, press down gently on each cookie ball to create a crisscross pattern.
9. **Bake** in the preheated oven for 10-12 minutes, or until the edges are lightly golden brown.
10. **Remove** from the oven and let the cookies cool on the baking sheet for a few minutes before transferring them to a wire rack to cool completely.
11. **Enjoy** your delicious homemade peanut butter cookies! These cookies are perfect for peanut butter lovers and make a wonderful treat for any occasion.

Feel free to adjust the baking time slightly for softer or crisper cookies according to your preference.

Red Velvet Cake

Ingredients:

For the cake:

- 2 1/2 cups all-purpose flour
- 1 1/2 cups granulated sugar
- 1 teaspoon baking soda
- 1 teaspoon baking powder
- 1 teaspoon salt
- 2 tablespoons unsweetened cocoa powder
- 1 cup vegetable oil
- 1 cup buttermilk, at room temperature
- 2 large eggs, at room temperature
- 2 tablespoons red food coloring
- 1 teaspoon vanilla extract
- 1 teaspoon white vinegar

For the cream cheese frosting:

- 16 ounces cream cheese, softened
- 1/2 cup unsalted butter, softened
- 4 cups powdered sugar, sifted
- 1 teaspoon vanilla extract

Instructions:

1. **Preheat** your oven to 350°F (175°C). Grease and flour two 9-inch round cake pans, or line them with parchment paper.
2. **In a large bowl**, sift together the flour, sugar, baking soda, baking powder, salt, and cocoa powder.
3. **In another large bowl**, whisk together the vegetable oil, buttermilk, eggs, red food coloring, vanilla extract, and white vinegar until smooth.
4. **Gradually add** the dry ingredients to the wet ingredients, mixing until well combined and the batter is smooth.
5. **Divide** the batter evenly between the prepared cake pans.
6. **Bake** in the preheated oven for 25-30 minutes, or until a toothpick inserted into the center comes out clean.
7. **Remove** from the oven and let the cakes cool in the pans for 10 minutes before transferring them to a wire rack to cool completely.
8. **While the cakes are cooling**, prepare the cream cheese frosting:
    - In a large bowl, beat together the softened cream cheese and butter until smooth and creamy.

- Gradually add the powdered sugar, one cup at a time, beating well after each addition.
- Stir in the vanilla extract until smooth and creamy.

9. **Once the cakes are completely cooled**, spread a layer of cream cheese frosting on top of one cake layer.
10. **Place the second cake layer** on top and frost the top and sides of the cake with the remaining cream cheese frosting.
11. **Optional:** Decorate the cake with red velvet cake crumbs, sprinkles, or additional frosting as desired.
12. **Chill** the cake in the refrigerator for at least 30 minutes before slicing and serving to allow the frosting to set.
13. **Enjoy** your homemade red velvet cake! It's perfect for birthdays, celebrations, or any special occasion.

Carrot Cake

Ingredients:

For the carrot cake:

- 2 cups all-purpose flour
- 2 teaspoons baking powder
- 1 1/2 teaspoons baking soda
- 1 teaspoon salt
- 2 teaspoons ground cinnamon
- 1/2 teaspoon ground nutmeg
- 1/2 teaspoon ground ginger
- 1 cup vegetable oil
- 1 cup granulated sugar
- 1 cup packed light brown sugar
- 4 large eggs
- 2 teaspoons vanilla extract
- 3 cups grated carrots (about 5-6 medium carrots)
- 1 cup crushed pineapple, drained
- 1 cup chopped walnuts or pecans (optional)

For the cream cheese frosting:

- 8 ounces cream cheese, softened
- 1/2 cup unsalted butter, softened
- 4 cups powdered sugar, sifted
- 1 teaspoon vanilla extract

Instructions:

1. **Preheat** your oven to 350°F (175°C). Grease and flour two 9-inch round cake pans, or line them with parchment paper.
2. **In a large bowl**, sift together the flour, baking powder, baking soda, salt, cinnamon, nutmeg, and ginger.
3. **In another large bowl**, whisk together the vegetable oil, granulated sugar, brown sugar, eggs, and vanilla extract until smooth and well combined.
4. **Gradually add** the dry ingredients to the wet ingredients, mixing until just combined.
5. **Fold in** the grated carrots, crushed pineapple, and chopped nuts (if using) until evenly distributed in the batter.
6. **Divide** the batter evenly between the prepared cake pans.
7. **Bake** in the preheated oven for 30-35 minutes, or until a toothpick inserted into the center comes out clean.
8. **Remove** from the oven and let the cakes cool in the pans for 10 minutes before transferring them to a wire rack to cool completely.

9. **While the cakes are cooling**, prepare the cream cheese frosting:
    - In a large bowl, beat together the softened cream cheese and butter until smooth and creamy.
    - Gradually add the powdered sugar, one cup at a time, beating well after each addition.
    - Stir in the vanilla extract until smooth and creamy.
10. **Once the cakes are completely cooled**, spread a layer of cream cheese frosting on top of one cake layer.
11. **Place the second cake layer** on top and frost the top and sides of the cake with the remaining cream cheese frosting.
12. **Optional:** Decorate the cake with chopped nuts, shredded carrots, or additional frosting as desired.
13. **Chill** the cake in the refrigerator for at least 30 minutes before slicing and serving to allow the frosting to set.
14. **Enjoy** your homemade carrot cake! It's perfect for gatherings, holidays, or any occasion where you want to impress with a moist and flavorful dessert.

Banana Bread

Ingredients:

- 2 to 3 ripe bananas, mashed (about 1 cup)
- 1/2 cup unsalted butter, melted
- 1/2 cup granulated sugar
- 1/2 cup packed light brown sugar
- 2 large eggs, beaten
- 1 teaspoon vanilla extract
- 1 1/2 cups all-purpose flour
- 1 teaspoon baking soda
- 1/2 teaspoon salt
- 1/2 teaspoon ground cinnamon (optional)
- 1/4 teaspoon ground nutmeg (optional)
- 1/2 cup chopped nuts (walnuts or pecans), chocolate chips, or dried fruit (optional)

Instructions:

1. **Preheat** your oven to 350°F (175°C). Grease a 9x5-inch loaf pan or line it with parchment paper.
2. In a mixing bowl, **mash the ripe bananas** with a fork or potato masher until smooth.
3. **Add the melted butter** to the mashed bananas and stir until well combined.
4. **Add the granulated sugar, brown sugar, eggs, and vanilla extract** to the banana mixture. Mix well until smooth.
5. **In a separate bowl**, whisk together the flour, baking soda, salt, cinnamon (if using), and nutmeg (if using).
6. **Gradually add** the dry ingredients to the wet ingredients, mixing until just combined. Do not overmix.
7. **Fold in** the chopped nuts, chocolate chips, or dried fruit (if using) until evenly distributed in the batter.
8. **Pour the batter** into the prepared loaf pan and smooth the top with a spatula.
9. **Bake** in the preheated oven for 60-70 minutes, or until a toothpick inserted into the center comes out clean.
10. **Remove** from the oven and let the banana bread cool in the pan for 10-15 minutes.
11. **Carefully transfer** the bread from the pan to a wire rack to cool completely before slicing.
12. **Slice** and serve your homemade banana bread, and enjoy it warm or at room temperature!

This banana bread is perfect for breakfast, brunch, or as a snack any time of day. It also freezes well, so you can make a double batch and save some for later.

Apple Pie

Ingredients:

For the pie crust:

- 2 1/2 cups all-purpose flour
- 1 teaspoon salt
- 1 tablespoon granulated sugar
- 1 cup unsalted butter, cold and cut into small cubes
- 6-8 tablespoons ice water

For the apple filling:

- 6-7 medium-sized apples (such as Granny Smith or Honeycrisp), peeled, cored, and thinly sliced
- 1/2 cup granulated sugar
- 1/4 cup packed light brown sugar
- 1 tablespoon lemon juice
- 1 teaspoon ground cinnamon
- 1/4 teaspoon ground nutmeg
- 1/4 teaspoon ground allspice (optional)
- 2 tablespoons unsalted butter, cut into small cubes
- 1 tablespoon all-purpose flour (optional, to thicken filling)

For assembling:

- 1 egg, beaten (for egg wash)
- 1 tablespoon granulated sugar (for sprinkling on top)

Instructions:

1. **Make the pie crust:**
    - In a large bowl, whisk together the flour, salt, and granulated sugar.
    - Add the cold cubed butter to the flour mixture. Use a pastry cutter or your fingertips to work the butter into the flour until it resembles coarse crumbs with some pea-sized pieces of butter remaining.
    - Gradually add the ice water, 1 tablespoon at a time, mixing with a fork until the dough begins to come together. You may need more or less water depending on humidity.
    - Divide the dough in half and shape each half into a disk. Wrap each disk tightly in plastic wrap and refrigerate for at least 1 hour, or overnight.
2. **Prepare the apple filling:**
    - In a large bowl, toss the sliced apples with lemon juice to prevent browning.
    - In a separate bowl, mix together the granulated sugar, brown sugar, cinnamon, nutmeg, and allspice (if using).

- Sprinkle the sugar mixture over the apples and toss until the apples are evenly coated. If your apples are very juicy, you can sprinkle 1 tablespoon of flour over the filling to help thicken it.
3. **Assemble the pie:**
    - Preheat your oven to 375°F (190°C). Place a baking sheet in the oven to preheat as well.
    - On a lightly floured surface, roll out one disk of chilled dough into a circle about 12 inches in diameter. Carefully transfer the dough to a 9-inch pie dish, gently pressing it into the bottom and sides.
    - Spoon the apple filling into the pie crust, mounding it slightly in the center. Dot the filling with cubes of butter.
4. **Roll out the second disk of dough** into a circle about 12 inches in diameter. Place it over the filling. Trim any excess dough from the edges and crimp the edges together using your fingers or a fork.
5. **Cut slits** in the top crust to allow steam to escape during baking. Optionally, you can brush the top crust with an egg wash (beaten egg mixed with a tablespoon of water) and sprinkle with granulated sugar for a golden, shiny crust.
6. **Place the pie** on the preheated baking sheet in the oven and bake for 45-55 minutes, or until the crust is golden brown and the filling is bubbling. If the edges of the crust start to brown too quickly, cover them loosely with aluminum foil.
7. **Remove** the pie from the oven and let it cool on a wire rack for at least 2 hours before slicing and serving. This helps the filling set.
8. **Serve** your homemade apple pie warm or at room temperature, optionally with a scoop of vanilla ice cream or a dollop of whipped cream.

Enjoy this classic apple pie with its buttery, flaky crust and flavorful apple filling—perfect for any occasion, especially during the fall season!

Cheesecake

Ingredients:

For the crust:

- 1 1/2 cups graham cracker crumbs (about 12-14 graham crackers)
- 1/4 cup granulated sugar
- 1/2 cup unsalted butter, melted

For the cheesecake filling:

- 4 packages (8 ounces each) cream cheese, softened
- 1 cup granulated sugar
- 1 teaspoon vanilla extract
- 4 large eggs, at room temperature
- 1 cup sour cream, at room temperature

Instructions:

1. **Preheat** your oven to 325°F (160°C). Grease a 9-inch springform pan.
2. **Make the crust:**
    - In a medium bowl, combine the graham cracker crumbs, granulated sugar, and melted butter. Mix until the crumbs are evenly moistened.
    - Press the mixture evenly into the bottom of the prepared springform pan.
    - Bake the crust in the preheated oven for 10 minutes. Remove from the oven and let it cool while preparing the filling.
3. **Make the cheesecake filling:**
    - In a large bowl, beat the softened cream cheese and granulated sugar until smooth and creamy, using a hand mixer or stand mixer with paddle attachment.
    - Mix in the vanilla extract.
    - Add the eggs one at a time, mixing well after each addition. Scrape down the sides of the bowl as needed.
    - Stir in the sour cream until smooth and well combined.
4. **Pour the filling** over the cooled crust in the springform pan. Smooth the top with a spatula.
5. **Bake the cheesecake** in the preheated oven for 45-55 minutes, or until the edges are set and the center is slightly jiggly.
6. **Turn off the oven** and prop open the oven door slightly. Let the cheesecake cool in the oven for 1 hour.
7. **Remove the cheesecake** from the oven and run a knife around the edges of the pan to loosen the cheesecake from the sides.
8. **Chill the cheesecake** in the refrigerator for at least 4 hours, preferably overnight, to set completely.

9. **Before serving,** carefully remove the sides of the springform pan. Slice and serve your cheesecake plain or with your favorite toppings such as fruit compote, chocolate sauce, or whipped cream.
10. **Enjoy** your homemade cheesecake! It's perfect for special occasions or as a delightful dessert any time.

This classic cheesecake recipe results in a smooth and creamy texture with a rich, tangy flavor that's sure to impress your family and friends.

Cinnamon Rolls

Ingredients:

For the dough:

- 1 cup warm milk (about 110°F)
- 2 1/4 teaspoons active dry yeast (1 packet)
- 1/2 cup granulated sugar
- 1/3 cup unsalted butter, melted
- 2 large eggs, room temperature
- 4 1/2 cups all-purpose flour
- 1 teaspoon salt

For the filling:

- 1/2 cup unsalted butter, softened
- 1 cup packed light brown sugar
- 2 tablespoons ground cinnamon

For the cream cheese frosting:

- 4 ounces cream cheese, softened
- 1/4 cup unsalted butter, softened
- 1 cup powdered sugar, sifted
- 1/2 teaspoon vanilla extract

Instructions:

1. **Activate the yeast:**
   - In a small bowl, combine the warm milk, yeast, and a pinch of sugar. Let it sit for about 5-10 minutes until foamy.
2. **Make the dough:**
   - In a large bowl or the bowl of a stand mixer fitted with a dough hook, combine the activated yeast mixture, sugar, melted butter, eggs, flour, and salt.
   - Mix on low speed until the dough comes together.
   - Increase the speed to medium and knead the dough for 5-7 minutes until smooth and elastic. If kneading by hand, knead on a lightly floured surface for about 10 minutes.
   - Place the dough in a greased bowl, cover with a clean kitchen towel or plastic wrap, and let it rise in a warm place for 1-2 hours, or until doubled in size.
3. **Make the filling:**
   - In a small bowl, mix together the softened butter, brown sugar, and ground cinnamon until smooth and well combined.
4. **Assemble the cinnamon rolls:**

- Punch down the risen dough and roll it out on a lightly floured surface into a 16x21-inch rectangle.
- Spread the cinnamon filling evenly over the dough, leaving a 1-inch border around the edges.

5. **Roll up the dough:**
   - Starting with the long edge, tightly roll up the dough into a log.
   - Cut the log into 12 equal slices using a sharp knife or dental floss for clean cuts.
6. **Arrange in the pan:**
   - Place the cinnamon rolls in a greased 9x13-inch baking pan or two 9-inch round cake pans, with the cut sides facing up.
7. **Let rise again:**
   - Cover the pan(s) with a clean kitchen towel or plastic wrap and let the rolls rise in a warm place for 30-45 minutes, or until puffy and doubled in size.
8. **Bake the cinnamon rolls:**
   - Preheat your oven to 350°F (175°C).
   - Bake the rolls in the preheated oven for 25-30 minutes, or until golden brown.
9. **Make the cream cheese frosting:**
   - In a medium bowl, beat together the softened cream cheese and butter until smooth and creamy.
   - Gradually add the powdered sugar, beating well after each addition.
   - Stir in the vanilla extract until smooth.
10. **Frost the cinnamon rolls:**
    - Spread the cream cheese frosting over the warm cinnamon rolls as soon as they come out of the oven.
    - Allow the rolls to cool slightly before serving.
11. **Enjoy** your homemade cinnamon rolls warm and gooey, with a generous drizzle of cream cheese frosting!

These cinnamon rolls are perfect for breakfast, brunch, or as a special treat for any occasion. They're best enjoyed fresh but can be stored in an airtight container at room temperature for up to 2 days.

Snickerdoodle Cookies

Ingredients:

- 1 cup unsalted butter, softened
- 1 1/2 cups granulated sugar
- 2 large eggs
- 1 teaspoon vanilla extract
- 2 3/4 cups all-purpose flour
- 1 1/2 teaspoons cream of tartar
- 1/2 teaspoon baking soda
- 1/4 teaspoon salt

For rolling:

- 1/4 cup granulated sugar
- 1 tablespoon ground cinnamon

Instructions:

1. **Preheat** your oven to 375°F (190°C). Line baking sheets with parchment paper or silicone baking mats.
2. **In a large bowl**, cream together the softened butter and 1 1/2 cups granulated sugar until light and fluffy.
3. **Add the eggs** one at a time, mixing well after each addition. Stir in the vanilla extract.
4. **In a separate bowl**, whisk together the flour, cream of tartar, baking soda, and salt.
5. **Gradually add** the dry ingredients to the butter mixture, mixing until just combined. Do not overmix.
6. **In a small bowl**, mix together the 1/4 cup granulated sugar and ground cinnamon for rolling.
7. **Shape the dough** into 1-inch balls (about the size of a walnut) and roll each ball in the cinnamon-sugar mixture until coated.
8. **Place the coated balls** 2 inches apart on the prepared baking sheets.
9. **Bake** in the preheated oven for 8-10 minutes, or until the edges are lightly golden but the centers are still soft.
10. **Remove** from the oven and let the cookies cool on the baking sheets for 5 minutes before transferring them to a wire rack to cool completely.
11. **Enjoy** your homemade snickerdoodle cookies! They're best enjoyed fresh but can be stored in an airtight container at room temperature for several days.

These snickerdoodle cookies are perfect for holiday baking, parties, or any time you crave a cinnamon-sugar treat. They have a wonderful balance of softness and chewiness with a delightful cinnamon flavor.

Strawberry Shortcake

Ingredients:

For the biscuits:

- 2 cups all-purpose flour
- 1/4 cup granulated sugar
- 1 tablespoon baking powder
- 1/2 teaspoon salt
- 1/2 cup unsalted butter, cold and cut into small pieces
- 3/4 cup buttermilk (or milk with 1 tablespoon vinegar or lemon juice)

For the strawberries:

- 1 pound fresh strawberries, hulled and sliced
- 2-3 tablespoons granulated sugar (adjust to taste)
- 1 teaspoon vanilla extract (optional)

For the whipped cream:

- 1 cup heavy cream, chilled
- 2 tablespoons powdered sugar
- 1 teaspoon vanilla extract

Instructions:

1. **Preheat** your oven to 400°F (200°C). Line a baking sheet with parchment paper.
2. **Make the biscuits:**
   - In a large bowl, whisk together the flour, sugar, baking powder, and salt.
   - Cut in the cold butter using a pastry cutter or your fingers until the mixture resembles coarse crumbs.
   - Gradually add the buttermilk, stirring until the dough just comes together and forms a sticky mass.
   - Turn the dough out onto a lightly floured surface and gently knead a few times until it holds together.
   - Pat the dough into a circle about 1-inch thick. Use a biscuit cutter or a glass to cut out rounds of dough. Place them on the prepared baking sheet.
   - Gather the remaining dough scraps, gently pat together, and cut out more rounds. Avoid overworking the dough.
3. **Bake the biscuits:**
   - Bake in the preheated oven for 12-15 minutes, or until the tops are golden brown. Remove from the oven and let them cool on a wire rack.
4. **Prepare the strawberries:**
   - In a bowl, toss the sliced strawberries with granulated sugar and vanilla extract (if using). Let them sit for at least 15-20 minutes to release their juices.

5. **Make the whipped cream:**
    - In a chilled bowl, whip the heavy cream with powdered sugar and vanilla extract until stiff peaks form.
6. **Assemble the strawberry shortcakes:**
    - Slice each biscuit in half horizontally.
    - Spoon a generous amount of strawberries with their juices onto the bottom half of each biscuit.
    - Dollop a generous amount of whipped cream over the strawberries.
    - Place the top half of the biscuit over the whipped cream.
7. **Serve** immediately and enjoy your homemade strawberry shortcake!

This dessert is best served fresh, allowing the biscuits to soak up some of the strawberry juices while maintaining their fluffiness. It's a perfect treat for summer gatherings or any occasion when you want to enjoy the sweet flavors of fresh strawberries and whipped cream.

Blueberry Muffins

Ingredients:

- 1/2 cup unsalted butter, melted and cooled slightly
- 1 cup granulated sugar
- 2 large eggs
- 1 teaspoon vanilla extract
- 1/2 cup milk
- 2 cups all-purpose flour
- 2 teaspoons baking powder
- 1/2 teaspoon salt
- 2 cups fresh or frozen blueberries (if using frozen, do not thaw)

For topping (optional):

- 2 tablespoons granulated sugar
- 1/2 teaspoon ground cinnamon

Instructions:

1. **Preheat** your oven to 375°F (190°C). Line a muffin tin with paper liners or grease the muffin cups.
2. **In a large bowl**, whisk together the melted butter and sugar until well combined.
3. **Add the eggs** one at a time, beating well after each addition. Stir in the vanilla extract.
4. **Add the milk** and mix until smooth and creamy.
5. **In a separate bowl**, whisk together the flour, baking powder, and salt.
6. **Gradually add** the dry ingredients to the wet ingredients, mixing until just combined. Do not overmix; the batter should be thick and lumpy.
7. **Gently fold in** the blueberries until evenly distributed in the batter. Be careful not to crush the blueberries.
8. **Scoop the batter** into the prepared muffin tin, filling each cup about 2/3 full.
9. **If using topping:** In a small bowl, mix together the granulated sugar and ground cinnamon. Sprinkle this mixture evenly over the tops of the muffins.
10. **Bake** in the preheated oven for 18-20 minutes, or until the muffins are golden brown and a toothpick inserted into the center comes out clean.
11. **Remove** from the oven and let the muffins cool in the tin for 5 minutes before transferring them to a wire rack to cool completely.
12. **Serve** warm or at room temperature. Enjoy your homemade blueberry muffins!

These muffins are best enjoyed fresh on the day they are baked but can be stored in an airtight container at room temperature for up to 3 days. They're perfect for breakfast, brunch, or as a tasty snack any time of day.

Key Lime Pie

Ingredients:

For the graham cracker crust:

- 1 1/2 cups graham cracker crumbs (about 10-12 graham crackers)
- 1/3 cup granulated sugar
- 6 tablespoons unsalted butter, melted

For the key lime pie filling:

- 1 can (14 ounces) sweetened condensed milk
- 4 large egg yolks
- 1/2 cup key lime juice (freshly squeezed if possible)
- 1 tablespoon finely grated lime zest (from about 2 limes)

For garnish (optional):

- Whipped cream
- Lime slices
- Lime zest

Instructions:

1. **Preheat** your oven to 350°F (175°C).
2. **Make the graham cracker crust:**
    - In a medium bowl, combine the graham cracker crumbs and granulated sugar.
    - Add the melted butter and stir until the crumbs are evenly moistened.
    - Press the mixture firmly and evenly into the bottom and up the sides of a 9-inch pie dish.
3. **Bake the crust:**
    - Bake in the preheated oven for 8-10 minutes, or until the crust is set and lightly golden brown.
    - Remove from the oven and let it cool slightly while you prepare the filling. Keep the oven on.
4. **Make the key lime pie filling:**
    - In a large bowl, whisk together the sweetened condensed milk, egg yolks, key lime juice, and lime zest until smooth and well combined.
    - Pour the filling into the baked graham cracker crust, spreading it evenly.
5. **Bake the pie:**
    - Return the pie to the oven and bake for 15-17 minutes, or until the filling is set but still slightly jiggly in the center.
6. **Cool and chill the pie:**
    - Remove the pie from the oven and let it cool to room temperature on a wire rack.

- Once cooled, refrigerate the pie for at least 2 hours, preferably longer, until fully chilled and set.
7. **Serve the key lime pie:**
    - Before serving, optionally garnish with whipped cream, lime slices, and/or lime zest.
8. **Enjoy** your homemade key lime pie! It's tangy, creamy, and perfect for summer or any time you crave a refreshing dessert.

Key lime pie can be stored in the refrigerator, covered, for up to 3-4 days. The longer it chills, the more the flavors meld together, enhancing its deliciousness.

Tiramisu

Ingredients:

- 1 1/2 cups brewed strong coffee or espresso, cooled to room temperature
- 1/4 cup coffee liqueur (such as Kahlua), optional
- 24-30 ladyfinger cookies (savoiardi)
- 4 large eggs, separated
- 1 cup granulated sugar, divided
- 16 ounces (about 2 cups) mascarpone cheese, softened
- 1 teaspoon vanilla extract
- Cocoa powder, for dusting

Instructions:

1. **Prepare the coffee mixture:**
   - Brew the coffee or espresso and let it cool to room temperature. Stir in the coffee liqueur if using.
2. **Prepare the mascarpone mixture:**
   - In a large mixing bowl, beat the egg yolks with 1/2 cup of sugar until pale and creamy.
   - Add the mascarpone cheese and vanilla extract. Beat until smooth and well combined.
3. **Whip the egg whites:**
   - In a separate clean bowl, beat the egg whites until soft peaks form.
   - Gradually add the remaining 1/2 cup of sugar, beating until stiff peaks form.
4. **Combine the mixtures:**
   - Gently fold the whipped egg whites into the mascarpone mixture until fully incorporated. Be gentle to maintain the airy texture.
5. **Assemble the tiramisu:**
   - Quickly dip each ladyfinger cookie into the coffee mixture (do not soak too long to avoid them becoming soggy) and line them in a single layer in the bottom of a 9x13-inch dish or a similar sized serving dish.
   - Spread half of the mascarpone mixture over the soaked ladyfingers, smoothing it out evenly.
6. **Repeat the layers:**
   - Repeat with another layer of dipped ladyfingers and the remaining mascarpone mixture on top.
7. **Chill the tiramisu:**
   - Cover the tiramisu with plastic wrap and refrigerate for at least 4 hours, preferably overnight, to allow the flavors to meld and the dessert to set.
8. **Serve the tiramisu:**
   - Before serving, dust the top generously with cocoa powder using a fine-mesh sieve.

9. **Enjoy** your homemade tiramisu! It's best served chilled and makes a delightful ending to any meal.

Tiramisu can be stored in the refrigerator, covered, for up to 3-4 days. It's a perfect dessert for special occasions or when you want to impress with a classic Italian treat. Buon appetito!

Pecan Pie

Ingredients:

For the pie crust:

- 1 1/4 cups all-purpose flour
- 1/2 teaspoon salt
- 1/2 cup unsalted butter, cold and cut into small cubes
- 1/4 cup ice water (more or less as needed)

For the pecan pie filling:

- 1 cup granulated sugar
- 1 cup light corn syrup
- 1/3 cup unsalted butter, melted
- 3 large eggs, beaten
- 1 teaspoon vanilla extract
- 1/4 teaspoon salt
- 1 1/2 cups pecan halves

Instructions:

1. **Make the pie crust:**
    - In a large bowl, whisk together the flour and salt.
    - Add the cold butter cubes and using a pastry cutter or your fingers, work the butter into the flour until the mixture resembles coarse crumbs with some pea-sized pieces of butter.
    - Gradually add the ice water, 1 tablespoon at a time, mixing with a fork until the dough just begins to come together.
    - Gather the dough into a ball, flatten into a disk, wrap tightly in plastic wrap, and refrigerate for at least 1 hour, or overnight.
2. **Preheat** your oven to 375°F (190°C).
3. **Roll out the pie crust:**
    - On a lightly floured surface, roll out the chilled dough into a circle about 12 inches in diameter. Carefully transfer it to a 9-inch pie dish. Trim any excess dough hanging over the edges and crimp the edges decoratively. Place the pie dish in the refrigerator while you prepare the filling.
4. **Make the pecan pie filling:**
    - In a large bowl, whisk together the granulated sugar, corn syrup, melted butter, beaten eggs, vanilla extract, and salt until well combined.
    - Stir in the pecan halves until evenly coated.
5. **Assemble and bake the pie:**
    - Pour the pecan pie filling into the chilled pie crust.

- Place the pie on a baking sheet to catch any spills and bake in the preheated oven for 40-50 minutes, or until the filling is set and slightly puffed, and the crust is golden brown.
6. **Cool and serve:**
    - Remove the pie from the oven and let it cool completely on a wire rack before slicing and serving.
7. **Enjoy** your homemade pecan pie! Serve it at room temperature or slightly warmed, optionally topped with whipped cream or a scoop of vanilla ice cream.

Pecan pie is a wonderful dessert for holidays like Thanksgiving or any occasion when you want to enjoy a decadent, nutty treat. It can be stored at room temperature for up to 2 days, covered loosely with foil or plastic wrap.

Coconut Macaroons

Ingredients:

- 3 cups sweetened shredded coconut
- 1/2 cup sweetened condensed milk
- 1 teaspoon vanilla extract
- 2 large egg whites
- 1/4 teaspoon salt
- Optional: 4 ounces semi-sweet or dark chocolate, melted (for dipping)

Instructions:

1. **Preheat** your oven to 325°F (160°C). Line a baking sheet with parchment paper or a silicone baking mat.
2. **In a large bowl**, combine the sweetened shredded coconut, sweetened condensed milk, and vanilla extract. Mix until well combined.
3. **In a separate bowl**, using a hand mixer or stand mixer with a whisk attachment, beat the egg whites and salt until stiff peaks form.
4. **Gently fold** the beaten egg whites into the coconut mixture until evenly combined. Be careful not to deflate the egg whites too much.
5. **Using a spoon or cookie scoop**, drop rounded tablespoons of the mixture onto the prepared baking sheet, spacing them about 1 inch apart.
6. **Bake** in the preheated oven for 18-20 minutes, or until the edges of the macaroons are golden brown.
7. **Optional:** If dipping in chocolate, melt the chocolate in a microwave-safe bowl in 30-second intervals, stirring between each interval until smooth. Dip the cooled macaroons halfway into the melted chocolate and place them back on the baking sheet. Allow the chocolate to set at room temperature or in the refrigerator.
8. **Let the macaroons cool completely** on the baking sheet before serving or storing.
9. **Enjoy** your homemade coconut macaroons! They are chewy on the inside with a crispy exterior and make a perfect treat for coconut lovers.

These coconut macaroons can be stored in an airtight container at room temperature for several days. They are great for holiday gatherings, dessert tables, or as a sweet snack any time of the year.

Gingerbread Cookies

Ingredients:

- 3 cups all-purpose flour
- 1 teaspoon baking soda
- 1/4 teaspoon salt
- 1 tablespoon ground ginger
- 1 1/2 teaspoons ground cinnamon
- 1/2 teaspoon ground cloves
- 1/2 teaspoon ground nutmeg
- 3/4 cup unsalted butter, softened
- 1/2 cup granulated sugar
- 1/2 cup packed light brown sugar
- 1 large egg
- 1/2 cup molasses
- 1 teaspoon vanilla extract

For decorating (optional):

- Royal icing
- Sprinkles, colored sugar, or candies

Instructions:

1. **In a medium bowl**, whisk together the flour, baking soda, salt, ginger, cinnamon, cloves, and nutmeg until well combined. Set aside.
2. **In a large bowl** or the bowl of a stand mixer fitted with the paddle attachment, cream together the softened butter, granulated sugar, and brown sugar until light and fluffy.
3. **Add the egg**, molasses, and vanilla extract to the butter-sugar mixture. Beat until well combined.
4. **Gradually add** the dry ingredients to the wet ingredients, mixing on low speed until the dough comes together. If the dough is too sticky, you can add a little more flour, a tablespoon at a time, until it reaches a workable consistency.
5. **Divide the dough** into two equal portions, flatten each into a disk, wrap tightly in plastic wrap, and refrigerate for at least 1 hour or overnight. Chilling the dough helps it firm up and makes it easier to roll out.
6. **Preheat** your oven to 350°F (175°C). Line baking sheets with parchment paper or silicone baking mats.
7. **On a lightly floured surface**, roll out one disk of dough to about 1/4-inch thickness. Use gingerbread cookie cutters to cut out shapes. Place the cut-out cookies onto the prepared baking sheets, spacing them about 1 inch apart.
8. **Gather up the scraps**, reroll the dough, and continue cutting out cookies until all the dough is used.

9. **Bake** the cookies in the preheated oven for 8-10 minutes, or until the edges are set and the cookies are firm to the touch. Avoid overbaking to keep them soft and chewy.
10. **Remove** from the oven and let the cookies cool on the baking sheets for a few minutes before transferring them to a wire rack to cool completely.
11. **Decorate** the cooled gingerbread cookies with royal icing, sprinkles, colored sugar, or candies as desired. Allow the icing to set completely before storing or serving.
12. **Enjoy** your homemade gingerbread cookies! They're perfect for holiday parties, cookie exchanges, or as a festive treat with a cup of hot cocoa.

These gingerbread cookies can be stored in an airtight container at room temperature for up to a week. They also make wonderful gifts when packaged in decorative bags or boxes.

Raspberry Tart

Ingredients:

For the tart crust:

- 1 1/4 cups all-purpose flour
- 1/4 cup granulated sugar
- 1/4 teaspoon salt
- 1/2 cup unsalted butter, cold and cut into small cubes
- 1 large egg yolk
- 2 tablespoons ice water

For the almond cream (frangipane):

- 1/2 cup unsalted butter, softened
- 1/2 cup granulated sugar
- 1 cup almond flour (ground almonds)
- 1 tablespoon all-purpose flour
- 1 large egg
- 1 teaspoon vanilla extract

For assembling:

- 1 cup fresh raspberries
- 1/4 cup raspberry jam (for glazing)

Instructions:

1. **Make the tart crust:**
    - In a food processor, pulse together the flour, sugar, and salt until combined.
    - Add the cold cubed butter and pulse until the mixture resembles coarse crumbs.
    - In a small bowl, whisk together the egg yolk and ice water.
    - Gradually add the egg mixture to the flour mixture, pulsing until the dough just begins to come together.
    - Turn the dough out onto a lightly floured surface, knead gently until smooth, and shape it into a disk.
    - Wrap the dough in plastic wrap and refrigerate for at least 1 hour.
2. **Prepare the almond cream (frangipane):**
    - In a medium bowl, cream together the softened butter and granulated sugar until light and fluffy.
    - Add the almond flour, all-purpose flour, egg, and vanilla extract. Mix until well combined and smooth. Set aside.
3. **Preheat** your oven to 375°F (190°C). Lightly grease a 9-inch tart pan with a removable bottom.
4. **Roll out the tart crust:**

- On a lightly floured surface, roll out the chilled dough into a circle about 1/8-inch thick.
 - Carefully transfer the dough to the tart pan, pressing it into the bottom and up the sides. Trim any excess dough.
5. **Spread the almond cream:**
 - Spread the prepared almond cream evenly over the bottom of the tart crust.
6. **Assemble the tart:**
 - Arrange the fresh raspberries on top of the almond cream in a single layer, pressing them gently into the cream.
7. **Bake the tart:**
 - Place the tart on a baking sheet (to catch any drips) and bake in the preheated oven for 30-35 minutes, or until the crust is golden brown and the almond cream is set.
 - If the crust edges brown too quickly, cover them loosely with foil halfway through baking.
8. **Glaze the tart:**
 - In a small saucepan, heat the raspberry jam over low heat until melted and smooth.
 - Brush the melted raspberry jam over the top of the warm tart to glaze the raspberries.
9. **Cool and serve:**
 - Allow the tart to cool in the pan on a wire rack for at least 30 minutes before removing it from the tart pan.
 - Serve the raspberry tart warm or at room temperature.
10. **Enjoy** your homemade raspberry tart! It's perfect for special occasions, afternoon tea, or any time you want to enjoy a delicious fruit-filled dessert.

This raspberry tart can be stored in the refrigerator, covered, for up to 3 days. The flavors meld together beautifully, making it even more delightful the next day.

S'mores Bars

Ingredients:

- 1/2 cup unsalted butter, melted
- 1/4 cup granulated sugar
- 1/2 cup packed light brown sugar
- 1 large egg
- 1 teaspoon vanilla extract
- 1 1/3 cups all-purpose flour
- 3/4 cup graham cracker crumbs (about 6-8 graham crackers)
- 1 teaspoon baking powder
- 1/4 teaspoon salt
- 1 1/2 cups mini marshmallows
- 1 1/2 cups milk chocolate chips or chunks
- Additional graham cracker pieces for topping (optional)

Instructions:

1. **Preheat** your oven to 350°F (175°C). Grease or line a 9x9-inch baking pan with parchment paper, leaving an overhang for easy removal.
2. **In a large bowl**, whisk together the melted butter, granulated sugar, and brown sugar until smooth.
3. **Add the egg and vanilla extract**, and whisk until well combined.
4. **In a separate bowl**, whisk together the flour, graham cracker crumbs, baking powder, and salt.
5. **Gradually add the dry ingredients** to the wet ingredients, mixing until just combined. The dough will be thick.
6. **Press about two-thirds** of the dough evenly into the bottom of the prepared baking pan.
7. **Layer the marshmallows** evenly over the dough in the pan.
8. **Sprinkle the chocolate chips** over the marshmallows.
9. **Crumble the remaining dough** evenly over the top of the marshmallows and chocolate chips. If desired, scatter additional graham cracker pieces over the top for extra texture.
10. **Bake** in the preheated oven for 25-30 minutes, or until the top is golden brown and the marshmallows are puffed and lightly toasted.
11. **Remove** from the oven and let cool completely in the pan on a wire rack.
12. **Once cooled**, lift the bars out of the pan using the parchment paper overhang and transfer them to a cutting board.
13. **Cut into squares** and serve. Enjoy your homemade s'mores bars!

These bars are best enjoyed fresh, but any leftovers can be stored in an airtight container at room temperature for a few days. They're perfect for picnics, parties, or whenever you're craving the classic flavors of s'mores in a convenient bar form.

Pumpkin Bread

Ingredients:

- 1 3/4 cups all-purpose flour
- 1 teaspoon baking soda
- 1/2 teaspoon baking powder
- 1 teaspoon ground cinnamon
- 1/2 teaspoon ground nutmeg
- 1/2 teaspoon ground cloves
- 1/2 teaspoon salt
- 1/2 cup unsalted butter, softened
- 1 1/4 cups granulated sugar
- 2 large eggs
- 1 cup canned pumpkin puree (not pumpkin pie filling)
- 1/2 teaspoon vanilla extract
- 1/3 cup water

Optional add-ins:

- 1/2 cup chopped nuts (such as walnuts or pecans)
- 1/2 cup chocolate chips or raisins

Instructions:

1. **Preheat** your oven to 350°F (175°C). Grease and flour a 9x5-inch loaf pan or line it with parchment paper for easy removal.
2. **In a medium bowl**, whisk together the flour, baking soda, baking powder, ground cinnamon, nutmeg, cloves, and salt until well combined. Set aside.
3. **In a large bowl** or the bowl of a stand mixer, cream together the softened butter and granulated sugar until light and fluffy.
4. **Add the eggs**, one at a time, beating well after each addition.
5. **Mix in the pumpkin puree** and vanilla extract until smooth.
6. **Gradually add the dry ingredients** to the wet ingredients, alternating with the water, beginning and ending with the dry ingredients. Mix until just combined.
7. **Fold in any optional add-ins** such as chopped nuts, chocolate chips, or raisins.
8. **Pour the batter** into the prepared loaf pan and spread it evenly with a spatula.
9. **Bake** in the preheated oven for 60-70 minutes, or until a toothpick inserted into the center comes out clean.
10. **Cool** the pumpkin bread in the pan on a wire rack for 10-15 minutes.
11. **Remove** the bread from the pan and allow it to cool completely on a wire rack before slicing.
12. **Slice** and serve your homemade pumpkin bread. It's delicious on its own or with a pat of butter!

This pumpkin bread can be stored at room temperature in an airtight container or wrapped tightly in plastic wrap for up to 3-4 days. It also freezes well for longer storage. Enjoy it for breakfast, as a snack, or as a comforting dessert throughout the autumn season!

Almond Biscotti

Ingredients:

- 2 cups all-purpose flour
- 1 teaspoon baking powder
- 1/4 teaspoon salt
- 3/4 cup granulated sugar
- 1/2 cup unsalted butter, softened
- 2 large eggs
- 1 teaspoon vanilla extract
- 1/2 teaspoon almond extract
- 1 cup whole almonds, toasted and coarsely chopped

Optional for dipping:

- 4 ounces semi-sweet or dark chocolate, melted

Instructions:

1. **Preheat** your oven to 350°F (175°C). Line a baking sheet with parchment paper or a silicone baking mat.
2. **In a medium bowl**, whisk together the flour, baking powder, and salt until well combined. Set aside.
3. **In a large bowl** or the bowl of a stand mixer, cream together the softened butter and granulated sugar until light and fluffy.
4. **Add the eggs**, one at a time, beating well after each addition.
5. **Mix in the vanilla extract** and almond extract until combined.
6. **Gradually add** the dry ingredients to the wet ingredients, mixing until just combined.
7. **Fold in the toasted and chopped almonds** until evenly distributed throughout the dough.
8. **Divide the dough** in half. On a lightly floured surface, shape each half into a log about 12 inches long and 2 inches wide. Place the logs on the prepared baking sheet, spacing them a few inches apart.
9. **Bake** in the preheated oven for 25-30 minutes, or until the logs are lightly golden brown and firm to the touch.
10. **Remove** the baking sheet from the oven and let the logs cool on the pan for 10-15 minutes. Reduce the oven temperature to 325°F (160°C).
11. **Carefully transfer** the cooled logs to a cutting board. Using a sharp serrated knife, cut the logs diagonally into 1/2-inch thick slices.
12. **Arrange the biscotti** cut side down on the baking sheet. Return them to the oven and bake for an additional 10-12 minutes, or until the biscotti are crisp and golden brown.
13. **Optional:** Let the biscotti cool completely. If desired, drizzle or dip them in melted chocolate and let the chocolate set before serving.

14. **Enjoy** your homemade almond biscotti! Store them in an airtight container at room temperature for up to 2 weeks. They make a perfect accompaniment to coffee, tea, or as a thoughtful gift.

These almond biscotti are crunchy on the outside and slightly chewy on the inside, with a wonderful almond flavor that complements their crispy texture.

Pineapple Upside-Down Cake

Ingredients:

For the topping:

- 1/4 cup unsalted butter
- 2/3 cup packed light brown sugar
- 1 can (20 ounces) pineapple slices in juice, drained (reserve juice)
- Maraschino cherries, drained and patted dry

For the cake batter:

- 1 1/2 cups all-purpose flour
- 1 1/2 teaspoons baking powder
- 1/4 teaspoon salt
- 1/2 cup unsalted butter, softened
- 3/4 cup granulated sugar
- 2 large eggs
- 1 teaspoon vanilla extract
- 1/2 cup pineapple juice (reserved from canned pineapple)
- 1/4 cup milk

Instructions:

1. **Preheat** your oven to 350°F (175°C). Grease a 9-inch round cake pan.
2. **Make the topping:**
    - In a small saucepan, melt the butter over medium heat.
    - Add the brown sugar and stir until dissolved and bubbly, about 2-3 minutes.
    - Pour the mixture into the prepared cake pan, spreading it evenly over the bottom.
3. **Arrange the pineapple slices** over the brown sugar mixture in a single layer. Place a maraschino cherry in the center of each pineapple slice and in any gaps between slices. Set aside.
4. **Make the cake batter:**
    - In a medium bowl, whisk together the flour, baking powder, and salt. Set aside.
    - In a large bowl or the bowl of a stand mixer, cream together the softened butter and granulated sugar until light and fluffy.
    - Add the eggs one at a time, beating well after each addition. Mix in the vanilla extract.
5. **Combine the wet and dry ingredients:**
    - Gradually add the dry ingredients to the creamed mixture, alternating with the pineapple juice and milk. Begin and end with the dry ingredients, mixing until just combined after each addition. Be careful not to overmix.
6. **Spread the batter** evenly over the pineapple slices and cherries in the cake pan, smoothing the top with a spatula.

7. **Bake** in the preheated oven for 40-45 minutes, or until a toothpick inserted into the center of the cake comes out clean.
8. **Cooling and serving:**
    - Remove the cake from the oven and let it cool in the pan for 10 minutes.
    - Run a knife around the edge of the cake to loosen it from the pan. Place a serving plate upside-down over the cake pan, then carefully invert the cake onto the plate. Remove the cake pan.
9. **Serve** the pineapple upside-down cake warm or at room temperature. Enjoy!

This pineapple upside-down cake is moist, flavorful, and has a beautiful presentation with its caramelized pineapple and cherries on top. It's a perfect dessert for any occasion and is sure to impress your guests!

Chocolate Eclairs

Ingredients:

For the choux pastry:

- 1/2 cup water
- 1/2 cup whole milk
- 1/2 cup unsalted butter, cut into cubes
- 1 tablespoon granulated sugar
- 1/4 teaspoon salt
- 1 cup all-purpose flour
- 4 large eggs, room temperature

For the pastry cream filling:

- 1 1/2 cups whole milk
- 1/2 cup granulated sugar
- 3 large egg yolks
- 1/4 cup cornstarch
- 1 teaspoon vanilla extract

For the chocolate ganache:

- 1/2 cup heavy cream
- 4 ounces semi-sweet or dark chocolate, finely chopped

Instructions:

1. **Make the choux pastry:**
    - Preheat your oven to 400°F (200°C). Line a baking sheet with parchment paper or a silicone baking mat.
    - In a medium saucepan, combine water, milk, butter, sugar, and salt. Bring to a boil over medium heat, stirring occasionally.
    - Once boiling, add the flour all at once. Stir vigorously with a wooden spoon until the mixture forms a ball and pulls away from the sides of the pan.
    - Transfer the dough to a mixing bowl and let it cool for 5 minutes.
    - Using a hand mixer or stand mixer fitted with a paddle attachment, beat the dough on low speed for 1-2 minutes to release steam and cool it slightly.
    - Add the eggs one at a time, beating well after each addition. The dough should be smooth and shiny, and it should hold its shape when piped.
2. **Pipe and bake the eclairs:**
    - Transfer the choux pastry dough to a piping bag fitted with a large round tip (about 1/2 inch in diameter).
    - Pipe 4-5 inch long strips onto the prepared baking sheet, leaving space between each eclair.

- Smooth down any peaks with a wet finger.
- Bake in the preheated oven for 15 minutes, then reduce the oven temperature to 350°F (175°C) and bake for an additional 25-30 minutes, or until the eclairs are golden brown and puffed.
- Remove from the oven and pierce each eclair with a skewer to release steam. Let them cool completely on a wire rack.

3. **Make the pastry cream filling:**
   - In a medium saucepan, heat the milk until steaming (do not boil).
   - In a separate bowl, whisk together the sugar, egg yolks, and cornstarch until smooth and pale.
   - Gradually whisk the hot milk into the egg mixture, then return the mixture to the saucepan.
   - Cook over medium heat, whisking constantly, until thickened and bubbling.
   - Remove from heat and stir in the vanilla extract.
   - Transfer the pastry cream to a bowl, cover with plastic wrap (directly on the surface to prevent a skin from forming), and chill in the refrigerator until cold.

4. **Fill the eclairs:**
   - Once the eclairs and pastry cream are completely cooled, use a sharp knife to cut each eclair horizontally, splitting them open.
   - Fill a piping bag fitted with a small round tip with the chilled pastry cream.
   - Pipe the pastry cream into each eclair until they feel full and slightly heavy.

5. **Make the chocolate ganache:**
   - In a small saucepan, heat the heavy cream until it just begins to simmer (do not boil).
   - Remove from heat and add the chopped chocolate. Let it sit for 1-2 minutes, then stir until smooth and glossy.

6. **Glaze the eclairs:**
   - Dip the top of each filled eclair into the chocolate ganache, allowing any excess to drip off.
   - Place the glazed eclairs on a wire rack to set the ganache for a few minutes.

7. **Serve and enjoy!**
   - Once the chocolate ganache is set, serve the chocolate eclairs immediately for best taste and texture.

Chocolate eclairs are best enjoyed fresh but can be stored in the refrigerator for up to 2-3 days. They are a delightful pastry that combines the rich flavors of chocolate and creamy custard, perfect for special occasions or as a decadent treat any time!

Coffee Cake

Ingredients:

For the streusel topping:

- 1/2 cup all-purpose flour
- 1/2 cup packed light brown sugar
- 1 teaspoon ground cinnamon
- 1/4 cup unsalted butter, melted

For the cake batter:

- 2 cups all-purpose flour
- 1 teaspoon baking powder
- 1 teaspoon baking soda
- 1/2 teaspoon salt
- 1/2 cup unsalted butter, softened
- 1 cup granulated sugar
- 2 large eggs
- 1 teaspoon vanilla extract
- 1 cup sour cream or plain Greek yogurt

For optional glaze:

- 1/2 cup powdered sugar
- 1-2 tablespoons milk or cream

Instructions:

1. **Preheat** your oven to 350°F (175°C). Grease and flour a 9x9-inch baking pan or line it with parchment paper.
2. **Make the streusel topping:**
    - In a small bowl, combine the flour, brown sugar, and cinnamon.
    - Pour in the melted butter and mix with a fork until crumbly. Set aside.
3. **Make the cake batter:**
    - In a medium bowl, whisk together the flour, baking powder, baking soda, and salt. Set aside.
    - In a large bowl or the bowl of a stand mixer, cream together the softened butter and granulated sugar until light and fluffy.
    - Add the eggs one at a time, beating well after each addition.
    - Mix in the vanilla extract.
4. **Alternate adding the dry ingredients** and sour cream (or yogurt) to the creamed mixture, beginning and ending with the dry ingredients. Mix until just combined, being careful not to overmix.
5. **Assemble the coffee cake:**

- Spread half of the cake batter into the prepared baking pan, smoothing it with a spatula.
- Sprinkle half of the streusel topping evenly over the batter.
- Dollop the remaining batter over the streusel and carefully spread it to cover the streusel layer.
- Sprinkle the remaining streusel topping evenly over the top.

6. **Bake** in the preheated oven for 35-40 minutes, or until a toothpick inserted into the center comes out clean and the top is golden brown.
7. **Optional glaze:**
    - In a small bowl, whisk together the powdered sugar and milk or cream until smooth.
    - Drizzle the glaze over the warm coffee cake.
8. **Cool and serve:**
    - Let the coffee cake cool in the pan on a wire rack for at least 15-20 minutes before slicing and serving.
9. **Enjoy** your homemade coffee cake! Serve warm or at room temperature with a hot cup of coffee or tea.

This coffee cake is moist, tender, and has a delightful cinnamon streusel topping that adds a perfect crunch. It's great for breakfast, brunch, or as a comforting dessert. Store any leftovers in an airtight container at room temperature for a few days.

Creme Brulee

Ingredients:

- 2 cups heavy cream
- 1 vanilla bean, split lengthwise (or 1 teaspoon vanilla extract)
- 5 large egg yolks
- 1/2 cup granulated sugar, plus extra for caramelizing

Instructions:

1. **Preheat** your oven to 325°F (160°C). Place 6 ramekins (4-6 oz size) in a deep baking dish.
2. **Prepare the custard:**
    - In a medium saucepan, combine the heavy cream and vanilla bean (scrape the seeds into the cream as well). Heat over medium heat until just simmering. Remove from heat and let it steep for 15-20 minutes to infuse the vanilla flavor. If using vanilla extract, add it after heating.
3. **Whisk together** the egg yolks and sugar in a large bowl until well combined and slightly thickened.
4. **Temper the eggs:** Slowly pour the warm cream mixture into the egg mixture, whisking constantly, until fully incorporated. Strain the custard through a fine-mesh sieve into a clean bowl or pitcher to remove any solids.
5. **Pour the custard** evenly into the ramekins, filling them almost to the top.
6. **Bake the custards:**
    - Carefully pour hot water into the baking dish around the ramekins, creating a water bath (about halfway up the sides of the ramekins).
    - Bake in the preheated oven for 30-35 minutes, or until the edges are set but the center still jiggles slightly when shaken.
7. **Chill the custards:**
    - Remove the ramekins from the water bath and let them cool to room temperature.
    - Cover each ramekin with plastic wrap (pressing it directly onto the surface of the custard) and refrigerate for at least 2 hours, or up to 2 days, to chill and set completely.
8. **Caramelize the sugar:**
    - Just before serving, sprinkle a thin, even layer of granulated sugar over the top of each custard.
    - Use a kitchen torch to caramelize the sugar: Hold the torch about 2 inches away from the sugar and move it in circular motions until the sugar melts and caramelizes to a golden brown color. Alternatively, place the ramekins under a broiler set to high for 1-2 minutes, watching carefully to avoid burning.
9. **Serve immediately:** Let the crème brûlée sit for a few minutes to allow the caramelized sugar to harden before serving.

10. **Enjoy** your homemade crème brûlée! The contrast between the creamy custard and the crunchy caramelized sugar makes it a delightfully indulgent dessert.

Crème brûlée is best served fresh after caramelizing the sugar, as the crispy topping can soften over time. It's a perfect dessert for special occasions or to impress guests with its elegant presentation and rich flavor.

Rice Krispie Treats

Ingredients:

- 6 cups crispy rice cereal (such as Rice Krispies)
- 1/4 cup unsalted butter
- 1 package (10 ounces) marshmallows (about 40 marshmallows)
- Optional: 1/2 teaspoon vanilla extract

Instructions:

1. **Prepare the pan:**
   - Lightly butter a 9x13-inch baking dish or line it with parchment paper.
2. **Melt the butter and marshmallows:**
   - In a large saucepan, melt the butter over low heat.
3. **Add the marshmallows:**
   - Once the butter is melted, add the marshmallows to the saucepan. Stir continuously until the marshmallows are completely melted and smooth. If using vanilla extract, stir it in after the marshmallows are melted.
4. **Combine with cereal:**
   - Remove the saucepan from heat and quickly add the crispy rice cereal to the melted marshmallow mixture. Stir until the cereal is evenly coated with the marshmallow mixture.
5. **Press into pan:**
   - Immediately transfer the mixture to the prepared baking dish. Use a buttered spatula or wax paper to press the mixture firmly and evenly into the pan.
6. **Cool and cut:**
   - Let the Rice Krispie Treats cool at room temperature for at least 30 minutes, or until set.
   - Once cooled and set, cut into squares or rectangles using a sharp knife.
7. **Serve and enjoy:**
   - Serve the Rice Krispie Treats at room temperature. They can be stored in an airtight container at room temperature for up to 2 days.

Variations:

- **Chocolate Drizzle:** Melt some chocolate chips and drizzle it over the cooled Rice Krispie Treats.
- **Peanut Butter:** Add 1/2 cup of creamy peanut butter to the marshmallow mixture for a peanut buttery twist.
- **Sprinkles:** Mix colorful sprinkles into the cereal mixture before pressing into the pan for a festive look.

Rice Krispie Treats are a nostalgic and crowd-pleasing dessert that's loved by kids and adults alike. They are quick to make and perfect for parties, school treats, or just a sweet snack any day of the week!

Meringue Cookies

Ingredients:

- 4 large egg whites, at room temperature
- 1 cup granulated sugar
- 1/4 teaspoon cream of tartar (optional, but helps stabilize the egg whites)
- 1/2 teaspoon vanilla extract (optional, for flavor)

Instructions:

1. **Preheat** your oven to 225°F (110°C). Line two baking sheets with parchment paper or silicone baking mats.
2. **Prepare the egg whites:**
   - In a clean, dry mixing bowl (preferably metal or glass), beat the egg whites on medium speed until frothy.
3. **Add cream of tartar (if using):**
   - Once the egg whites are frothy, add the cream of tartar. This helps stabilize the egg whites and gives the meringues a better structure.
4. **Gradually add sugar:**
   - With the mixer running on medium-high speed, gradually add the granulated sugar, about 1 tablespoon at a time. Continue beating until the sugar is completely dissolved and the egg whites form stiff, glossy peaks. This can take about 5-7 minutes.
5. **Add vanilla extract (if using):**
   - Gently fold in the vanilla extract, if desired, for flavoring.
6. **Pipe or spoon the meringue:**
   - Transfer the meringue mixture to a piping bag fitted with a large star or round tip, or simply use a spoon to drop dollops onto the prepared baking sheets.
7. **Bake the meringue cookies:**
   - Bake in the preheated oven for 1 to 1.5 hours, or until the meringue cookies are dry, crisp, and easily lift off the parchment paper. The baking time may vary depending on the size of your meringues and your oven. They should not brown.
8. **Cooling:**
   - Once baked, turn off the oven and leave the meringue cookies in the oven with the door slightly ajar for about 1 hour to cool and continue drying out.
9. **Serve and store:**
   - Once completely cooled and crisp, store the meringue cookies in an airtight container at room temperature. They can be kept for several days.

Tips for success:

- Ensure that your mixing bowl and beaters are clean and completely grease-free, as any trace of fat can prevent the egg whites from whipping properly.

- Be patient when adding the sugar; adding it gradually allows it to dissolve properly into the egg whites, resulting in a smooth and stable meringue.
- Experiment with flavors and colors by adding extracts (like almond or lemon) or food coloring to the meringue mixture before piping.

Meringue cookies are delightful on their own, but they can also be used to decorate cakes and desserts, or enjoyed alongside a cup of tea or coffee. They are low in fat and calories, making them a lighter sweet treat option.

Orange Sorbet

Ingredients:

- 1 cup water
- 1 cup granulated sugar
- 1 cup freshly squeezed orange juice (from about 4-5 large oranges)
- Zest of 1 orange
- 1-2 tablespoons freshly squeezed lemon juice (optional, to enhance citrus flavor)

Instructions:

1. **Make simple syrup:**
    - In a small saucepan, combine the water and granulated sugar. Heat over medium-high heat, stirring occasionally, until the sugar completely dissolves and the mixture comes to a gentle boil. Remove from heat and let it cool to room temperature. This is your simple syrup.
2. **Prepare the orange mixture:**
    - In a mixing bowl, combine the freshly squeezed orange juice, orange zest, and optional lemon juice (if using). Stir to mix well.
3. **Combine and chill:**
    - Pour the cooled simple syrup into the orange juice mixture. Stir until thoroughly combined.
4. **Chill the mixture:**
    - Cover the bowl with plastic wrap and refrigerate for at least 2 hours, or until thoroughly chilled. This step ensures that the sorbet freezes properly and evenly.
5. **Churn the sorbet:**
    - Once chilled, pour the orange mixture into an ice cream maker. Churn according to the manufacturer's instructions until the mixture reaches a sorbet-like consistency. It should be firm but still scoopable.
6. **Freeze the sorbet:**
    - Transfer the churned sorbet into a freezer-safe container. Smooth the top with a spatula and cover tightly with a lid or plastic wrap.
7. **Final freeze:**
    - Freeze the sorbet for at least 4 hours, or until firm.
8. **Serve and enjoy:**
    - Scoop the orange sorbet into bowls or glasses. Garnish with fresh orange slices or mint leaves, if desired.

Tips:

- For best results, use freshly squeezed orange juice. The zest adds extra citrus flavor and aroma.
- Adjust the sweetness to your liking by tasting the mixture before churning. You can add more or less simple syrup depending on how sweet your oranges are.

- If you don't have an ice cream maker, you can pour the mixture into a shallow baking dish, cover it with plastic wrap, and place it in the freezer. Stir the mixture every 30 minutes until it reaches the desired consistency.

Homemade orange sorbet is a delightful treat that captures the bright and tangy flavors of fresh oranges. It's dairy-free, vegan-friendly, and a perfect palate cleanser or dessert on a warm day.

Peanut Brittle

Ingredients:

- 1 cup granulated sugar
- 1/2 cup light corn syrup
- 1/4 cup water
- 1 cup roasted peanuts (unsalted)
- 2 tablespoons unsalted butter
- 1 teaspoon vanilla extract
- 1 teaspoon baking soda

Instructions:

1. **Prepare a baking sheet:**
    - Line a baking sheet with parchment paper or a silicone baking mat. Set aside.
2. **Combine sugar, corn syrup, and water:**
    - In a heavy-bottomed saucepan, combine the sugar, corn syrup, and water. Stir over medium heat until the sugar dissolves.
3. **Cook the sugar mixture:**
    - Bring the mixture to a boil. Insert a candy thermometer into the saucepan and continue to cook without stirring until the temperature reaches 300°F (150°C), also known as the hard crack stage. This will take about 10-15 minutes.
4. **Add peanuts and butter:**
    - Once the mixture reaches 300°F (150°C), immediately stir in the peanuts and butter. Stir constantly until the mixture reaches 280°F (140°C).
5. **Add vanilla and baking soda:**
    - Remove the saucepan from heat and quickly stir in the vanilla extract and baking soda. The mixture will bubble up and become frothy.
6. **Spread the mixture:**
    - Pour the hot mixture onto the prepared baking sheet. Use a spatula or wooden spoon to spread it out evenly into a thin layer. Work quickly as the mixture will begin to harden fast.
7. **Cool and break into pieces:**
    - Let the peanut brittle cool completely at room temperature until hardened, about 30-45 minutes.
    - Once cooled, break the brittle into pieces using your hands or a kitchen mallet.
8. **Store:**
    - Store the peanut brittle in an airtight container at room temperature. It will keep well for up to 2 weeks.

Tips:

- Be cautious when working with hot sugar as it can cause severe burns. Use a candy thermometer and handle the mixture carefully.

- Roasted peanuts are typically used for peanut brittle, but you can use raw peanuts and roast them yourself if desired.
- Customize your brittle by adding spices like cinnamon or a pinch of cayenne pepper for a kick.

Homemade peanut brittle makes a wonderful homemade gift or a sweet treat for holiday gatherings. Enjoy its crunchy texture and rich flavor!

Fig Newtons

Ingredients:

For the fig filling:

- 1 1/2 cups dried figs, stemmed and chopped
- 1/2 cup water
- Zest and juice of 1 lemon
- 1/4 cup honey or granulated sugar

For the cookie dough:

- 1 1/2 cups all-purpose flour
- 1/2 teaspoon baking powder
- 1/4 teaspoon salt
- 1/2 cup unsalted butter, softened
- 1/2 cup granulated sugar
- 1 large egg
- 1 teaspoon vanilla extract

Instructions:

1. **Make the fig filling:**
   - In a small saucepan, combine the chopped figs, water, lemon zest, lemon juice, and honey or sugar.
   - Bring to a simmer over medium heat, stirring occasionally.
   - Reduce the heat to low and cook for about 10-15 minutes, or until the figs are softened and the mixture thickens. Remove from heat and let it cool slightly.
2. **Blend the fig filling:**
   - Transfer the fig mixture to a food processor or blender. Blend until smooth. If needed, add a little water (1-2 tablespoons at a time) to achieve a spreadable consistency. Set aside to cool completely.
3. **Make the cookie dough:**
   - In a medium bowl, whisk together the flour, baking powder, and salt. Set aside.
   - In a large bowl or the bowl of a stand mixer, beat the softened butter and granulated sugar until light and fluffy.
   - Add the egg and vanilla extract, and beat until well combined.
   - Gradually add the flour mixture to the butter mixture, mixing until a soft dough forms.
4. **Assemble the Fig Newtons:**
   - Preheat your oven to 350°F (175°C). Line a baking sheet with parchment paper.
   - Divide the cookie dough into two equal portions. Place one portion of dough on a lightly floured surface and roll it out into a rectangle about 1/4 inch thick.

- Spread half of the fig filling evenly over the rolled-out dough, leaving a small border around the edges.
- Carefully roll the dough lengthwise, enclosing the fig filling to form a log shape. Press gently to seal the edges.
- Transfer the log onto the prepared baking sheet. Repeat with the remaining dough and fig filling.

5. **Bake the Fig Newtons:**
   - Bake in the preheated oven for 20-25 minutes, or until the cookies are lightly golden brown.
6. **Cool and slice:**
   - Remove from the oven and let the cookies cool on the baking sheet for about 10 minutes.
   - Transfer the logs to a cutting board and slice each log diagonally into 1-inch thick slices while still warm.
7. **Serve and store:**
   - Allow the Fig Newtons to cool completely on a wire rack before serving.
   - Store in an airtight container at room temperature for up to 1 week. They can also be frozen for longer storage.

Homemade Fig Newtons are a delightful treat that combines the natural sweetness of figs with a soft cookie exterior. Enjoy them as a snack or dessert, and share with family and friends for a nostalgic treat!

Maple Pecan Bars

Ingredients:

For the crust:

- 1 1/2 cups all-purpose flour
- 1/2 cup unsalted butter, softened
- 1/4 cup granulated sugar
- Pinch of salt

For the filling:

- 1 cup pure maple syrup
- 1/2 cup packed light brown sugar
- 2 large eggs
- 2 tablespoons all-purpose flour
- 1/2 teaspoon vanilla extract
- 1/4 teaspoon salt
- 1 1/2 cups chopped pecans

Instructions:

1. **Preheat** your oven to 350°F (175°C). Grease or line a 9x9-inch baking pan with parchment paper, leaving an overhang on the sides for easy removal.
2. **Make the crust:**
    - In a medium bowl, combine the flour, softened butter, granulated sugar, and a pinch of salt. Mix until crumbly and well combined.
    - Press the mixture evenly into the bottom of the prepared baking pan.
3. **Bake the crust:**
    - Bake in the preheated oven for 15-18 minutes, or until the edges are lightly golden. Remove from the oven and set aside.
4. **Make the filling:**
    - In a medium bowl, whisk together the maple syrup, brown sugar, eggs, flour, vanilla extract, and salt until smooth.
    - Stir in the chopped pecans until evenly distributed.
5. **Assemble and bake the bars:**
    - Pour the filling mixture over the partially baked crust, spreading it evenly.
    - Return the pan to the oven and bake for 25-30 minutes, or until the filling is set and slightly firm to the touch.
6. **Cool and slice:**
    - Allow the maple pecan bars to cool completely in the pan on a wire rack.
    - Once cooled, lift the bars out of the pan using the parchment paper overhang.
    - Cut into squares or bars using a sharp knife.
7. **Serve and enjoy:**

- Serve the maple pecan bars at room temperature. They can be stored in an airtight container at room temperature for up to 3 days, or refrigerated for longer storage.

These maple pecan bars are rich, buttery, and filled with the wonderful flavors of maple syrup and toasted pecans. They make a delightful dessert for gatherings or a sweet treat for any occasion!

Nutella Crepes

Ingredients:

For the crepe batter:

- 1 cup all-purpose flour
- 2 large eggs
- 1 cup milk
- 1/4 cup water
- 2 tablespoons unsalted butter, melted
- 1 tablespoon granulated sugar
- 1/2 teaspoon vanilla extract
- Pinch of salt

For assembling:

- Nutella (or any chocolate hazelnut spread)
- Fresh berries (optional, for serving)
- Powdered sugar (optional, for dusting)

Instructions:

1. **Make the crepe batter:**
    - In a blender or mixing bowl, combine the flour, eggs, milk, water, melted butter, sugar, vanilla extract, and salt.
    - Blend or whisk until smooth and well combined. The batter should be thin and pourable. If needed, add a bit more milk or water to achieve the right consistency.
    - Let the batter rest for at least 15-30 minutes at room temperature. This allows the flour to fully hydrate and results in softer crepes.
2. **Cook the crepes:**
    - Heat a non-stick skillet or crepe pan over medium heat. Lightly grease the pan with butter or cooking spray.
    - Pour about 1/4 cup of batter into the hot pan, swirling it around to evenly coat the bottom in a thin layer.
    - Cook for about 1-2 minutes, or until the edges of the crepe start to lift from the pan and the bottom is lightly golden.
    - Carefully flip the crepe using a spatula and cook for another 1 minute on the other side.
    - Transfer the cooked crepe to a plate and cover with a clean kitchen towel to keep warm. Repeat with the remaining batter, stacking the cooked crepes on top of each other.
3. **Assemble the crepes:**
    - Spread a generous amount of Nutella (or chocolate hazelnut spread of your choice) over one half of each crepe.

        - Fold the crepe in half, then fold it in half again to form a triangle or roll it up into a cylinder shape.
        - Repeat with the remaining crepes and Nutella.
4. **Serve:**
        - Arrange the Nutella crepes on a serving platter.
        - Optionally, top with fresh berries and dust with powdered sugar.
        - Serve warm and enjoy immediately.

Nutella crepes are versatile and can be enjoyed for breakfast, brunch, or as a dessert. They are customizable with various fillings like sliced bananas, strawberries, whipped cream, or even a drizzle of caramel sauce. Enjoy the delicious combination of tender crepes and creamy Nutella filling!

Mint Chocolate Chip Ice Cream

Ingredients:

- 2 cups heavy cream
- 1 cup whole milk
- 3/4 cup granulated sugar
- Pinch of salt
- 1 teaspoon pure peppermint extract (adjust to taste)
- Green food coloring (optional, for color)
- 1 cup semi-sweet chocolate chips or chunks

Instructions:

1. **Prepare the ice cream base:**
    - In a medium saucepan, combine the heavy cream, whole milk, granulated sugar, and salt.
    - Heat the mixture over medium heat, stirring occasionally, until the sugar dissolves completely and the mixture is just about to simmer. Do not boil.
2. **Infuse with mint flavor:**
    - Remove the saucepan from heat. Stir in the peppermint extract. Taste and adjust the amount of peppermint extract based on your preference for mintiness.
    - If desired, add a few drops of green food coloring to achieve a minty green color. Stir well to combine.
3. **Chill the mixture:**
    - Pour the ice cream base into a heatproof bowl or container. Cover with plastic wrap, pressing it directly onto the surface of the mixture to prevent a skin from forming.
    - Chill the mixture in the refrigerator for at least 2 hours, or preferably overnight, until thoroughly chilled.
4. **Churn the ice cream:**
    - Once chilled, pour the mixture into your ice cream maker and churn according to the manufacturer's instructions until it reaches a soft-serve consistency.
5. **Add chocolate chips:**
    - In the last few minutes of churning, add the chocolate chips or chunks to the ice cream maker, allowing them to mix evenly throughout the ice cream.
6. **Transfer and freeze:**
    - Transfer the churned ice cream into a freezer-safe container. Fold in any remaining chocolate chips with a spoon or spatula for a more chunky texture, if desired.
    - Smooth the top of the ice cream, cover with a lid or plastic wrap, and freeze for at least 4 hours or until firm.
7. **Serve and enjoy:**
    - Once fully frozen, scoop the mint chocolate chip ice cream into bowls or cones.
    - Garnish with extra chocolate chips or fresh mint leaves, if desired.

- - Enjoy the refreshing and creamy homemade mint chocolate chip ice cream!

Tips:

- For a more intense mint flavor, you can steep fresh mint leaves in the cream and milk mixture while heating it, then strain before chilling.
- Make sure your ice cream maker bowl is properly frozen according to the manufacturer's instructions before churning.
- Store leftover ice cream in an airtight container in the freezer for up to 2 weeks. Allow it to soften for a few minutes at room temperature before scooping.

Homemade mint chocolate chip ice cream is a delightful treat that beats store-bought versions with its fresh flavor and creamy texture. It's perfect for hot summer days or as a special dessert any time of year!

Amaretto Truffles

Ingredients:

- 8 ounces dark chocolate, finely chopped (around 60-70% cocoa)
- 1/2 cup heavy cream
- 2 tablespoons unsalted butter, softened
- 2 tablespoons amaretto liqueur
- 1/2 teaspoon almond extract (optional, for extra almond flavor)
- Cocoa powder, for rolling
- Sliced almonds or edible gold dust (optional, for decoration)

Instructions:

1. **Prepare the chocolate mixture:**
   - Place the finely chopped dark chocolate in a heatproof bowl.
2. **Heat the cream:**
   - In a small saucepan, heat the heavy cream over medium heat until it just begins to simmer. Do not boil.
3. **Make the ganache:**
   - Pour the hot cream over the chopped chocolate. Let it sit for 1-2 minutes to soften the chocolate.
   - Gently stir the mixture with a spatula or whisk until the chocolate is completely melted and smooth.
4. **Add the butter and amaretto:**
   - Stir in the softened butter, amaretto liqueur, and almond extract (if using) until well combined. The mixture should be shiny and glossy.
5. **Chill the ganache:**
   - Cover the bowl with plastic wrap, pressing it directly onto the surface of the ganache to prevent a skin from forming.
   - Chill in the refrigerator for at least 2 hours, or until the ganache is firm enough to scoop.
6. **Shape the truffles:**
   - Once chilled and firm, use a teaspoon or melon baller to scoop out small portions of the ganache.
   - Roll each portion into a smooth ball between your palms. Place the rolled truffles on a parchment-lined baking sheet.
7. **Coat the truffles:**
   - Place the cocoa powder in a shallow bowl or plate.
   - Roll each truffle in the cocoa powder until evenly coated. Shake off any excess cocoa powder.
8. **Decorate (optional):**
   - If desired, lightly press a sliced almond onto the top of each truffle for decoration.
   - Alternatively, dust the truffles with edible gold dust for a festive touch.
9. **Chill and store:**

- Once all truffles are coated, chill them in the refrigerator for about 30 minutes to set.
10. **Serve and enjoy:**
    - Arrange the Amaretto truffles on a serving platter or in mini paper cups.
    - Serve chilled and enjoy the rich, almond-flavored chocolate goodness!

Tips:

- Use good quality dark chocolate for the best flavor. Aim for chocolate with 60-70% cocoa content.
- Adjust the amount of amaretto liqueur to taste, but be cautious not to add too much as it can affect the texture of the ganache.
- Store the truffles in an airtight container in the refrigerator for up to 1 week. Bring them to room temperature before serving for the best texture and flavor.

These homemade Amaretto truffles are perfect for special occasions or as a delightful homemade gift for friends and family. They combine the richness of dark chocolate with the distinct flavor of amaretto liqueur, creating a truly decadent treat.

Cranberry Pistachio Biscotti

Ingredients:

- 2 cups all-purpose flour
- 1 teaspoon baking powder
- 1/4 teaspoon salt
- 1/2 cup unsalted butter, softened
- 3/4 cup granulated sugar
- 2 large eggs
- 1 teaspoon vanilla extract
- 1/2 cup dried cranberries
- 1/2 cup shelled pistachios, coarsely chopped
- Zest of 1 orange (optional, for extra flavor)

Instructions:

1. **Preheat** your oven to 350°F (175°C). Line a baking sheet with parchment paper or a silicone baking mat.
2. **Prepare the dry ingredients:**
   - In a medium bowl, whisk together the flour, baking powder, and salt. Set aside.
3. **Cream the butter and sugar:**
   - In a large bowl or the bowl of a stand mixer, cream together the softened butter and granulated sugar until light and fluffy.
4. **Add eggs and vanilla:**
   - Beat in the eggs, one at a time, until well combined. Add the vanilla extract and mix until incorporated.
5. **Combine wet and dry ingredients:**
   - Gradually add the flour mixture to the butter mixture, mixing until a dough forms. The dough will be slightly sticky.
6. **Add cranberries, pistachios, and orange zest:**
   - Fold in the dried cranberries, chopped pistachios, and orange zest (if using), ensuring they are evenly distributed throughout the dough.
7. **Shape the dough:**
   - Divide the dough in half. On a lightly floured surface, shape each half into a log about 12 inches long and 2 inches wide. Place the logs on the prepared baking sheet, leaving space between them.
8. **Bake the biscotti logs:**
   - Bake in the preheated oven for 25-30 minutes, or until the logs are firm to the touch and lightly golden brown.
9. **Cool and slice:**
   - Remove the baking sheet from the oven and let the biscotti logs cool for 10-15 minutes.
   - Using a sharp knife, slice the logs diagonally into 1/2-inch thick slices.
10. **Bake again:**

- Arrange the biscotti slices cut-side down on the baking sheet. Return to the oven and bake for an additional 10-12 minutes, flipping the slices halfway through, until they are golden and crisp.

11. **Cool and store:**
    - Transfer the baked biscotti to a wire rack to cool completely.
    - Once cooled, store in an airtight container at room temperature. They will keep well for up to 2 weeks.
12. **Serve and enjoy:**
    - Serve the cranberry pistachio biscotti with a hot cup of coffee or tea, or package them as a delightful homemade gift.

Tips:

- For a more pronounced orange flavor, add 1-2 tablespoons of orange juice along with the vanilla extract.
- You can dip the cooled biscotti in melted white or dark chocolate for an extra indulgent touch.
- Feel free to adjust the amount of cranberries and pistachios to your preference.

Homemade cranberry pistachio biscotti is perfect for enjoying yourself or sharing with loved ones. Its crunchy texture and delicious flavors make it a favorite during the holiday season or any time of year!

Mango Sorbet

Ingredients:

- 4 cups ripe mango, peeled, pitted, and chopped (about 4 large mangoes)
- 1/2 cup granulated sugar (adjust to taste depending on the sweetness of your mangoes)
- 1/4 cup water
- 2 tablespoons fresh lime juice (about 1 lime)

Instructions:

1. **Prepare the mango:**
   - Peel the mangoes and remove the pits. Chop the mango flesh into chunks.
2. **Make the simple syrup:**
   - In a small saucepan, combine the granulated sugar and water over medium heat. Stir until the sugar dissolves completely and the mixture comes to a gentle simmer. Remove from heat and let it cool completely.
3. **Blend the mango mixture:**
   - In a blender or food processor, combine the chopped mango chunks, cooled simple syrup, and fresh lime juice.
   - Blend until smooth and creamy. Taste the mixture and adjust sweetness if needed by adding more sugar or lime juice.
4. **Chill the mixture:**
   - Transfer the mango mixture to a bowl or container. Cover and refrigerate for at least 2 hours, or until thoroughly chilled.
5. **Churn the sorbet:**
   - Once chilled, pour the mango mixture into your ice cream maker.
   - Churn according to the manufacturer's instructions until the sorbet reaches a soft-serve consistency, typically about 20-25 minutes.
6. **Serve or freeze:**
   - Serve the mango sorbet immediately for a softer texture, or transfer it to a freezer-safe container for a firmer consistency.
   - If freezing for later, cover the container with a lid or plastic wrap directly on the surface of the sorbet to prevent ice crystals from forming.
7. **Enjoy:**
   - Scoop the mango sorbet into bowls or cones.
   - Garnish with fresh mint leaves or a slice of lime, if desired.
   - Enjoy the refreshing and tropical flavors of homemade mango sorbet!

Tips:

- Choose ripe mangoes for the best flavor. They should be fragrant and slightly soft to the touch.
- If you prefer a smoother sorbet, you can strain the blended mixture through a fine mesh sieve before chilling.

- Experiment with other fruits or flavorings, such as coconut milk or mint, to create variations of this refreshing dessert.

Homemade mango sorbet is perfect for hot summer days or as a light and fruity dessert after a meal. Its vibrant color and tropical taste will be a hit with friends and family alike!

Black Forest Cake

Ingredients:

For the chocolate sponge cake:

- 1 3/4 cups all-purpose flour
- 2 cups granulated sugar
- 3/4 cup unsweetened cocoa powder
- 1 1/2 teaspoons baking powder
- 1 1/2 teaspoons baking soda
- 1 teaspoon salt
- 2 large eggs
- 1 cup whole milk
- 1/2 cup vegetable oil
- 2 teaspoons vanilla extract
- 1 cup boiling water

For the cherry filling:

- 2 cups pitted cherries (fresh or canned, drained)
- 1/4 cup granulated sugar
- 1 tablespoon cornstarch
- 1/4 cup water
- 1 tablespoon lemon juice

For the whipped cream frosting:

- 3 cups heavy cream, chilled
- 1/2 cup powdered sugar
- 1 teaspoon vanilla extract

For garnish:

- Chocolate shavings or curls
- Maraschino cherries (optional)

Instructions:

1. **Prepare the chocolate sponge cake:**
    - Preheat your oven to 350°F (175°C). Grease and flour two 9-inch round cake pans.
    - In a large bowl, sift together the flour, sugar, cocoa powder, baking powder, baking soda, and salt.
    - Add the eggs, milk, oil, and vanilla extract to the dry ingredients. Beat on medium speed until well combined.

- Reduce speed and carefully add the boiling water to the cake batter. Beat on high speed for about 1 minute to add air to the batter.
- Divide the batter evenly between the prepared cake pans.
- Bake for 30 to 35 minutes, or until a toothpick inserted into the center comes out clean.
- Remove from the oven and allow the cakes to cool in the pans for 10 minutes before transferring them to a wire rack to cool completely.

2. **Prepare the cherry filling:**
    - In a medium saucepan, combine the cherries, sugar, cornstarch, water, and lemon juice.
    - Cook over medium heat, stirring constantly, until the mixture thickens and comes to a boil.
    - Reduce heat and simmer for 2-3 minutes, stirring occasionally.
    - Remove from heat and let the cherry filling cool completely.

3. **Make the whipped cream frosting:**
    - In a chilled mixing bowl, whip the heavy cream, powdered sugar, and vanilla extract until stiff peaks form.

4. **Assemble the Black Forest Cake:**
    - Place one layer of chocolate sponge cake on a serving plate.
    - Spread a layer of whipped cream frosting over the cake layer.
    - Spoon half of the cherry filling evenly over the whipped cream.
    - Place the second layer of chocolate sponge cake on top and press gently.
    - Frost the top and sides of the cake with the remaining whipped cream frosting.
    - Pipe whipped cream rosettes on top if desired, and garnish with chocolate shavings or curls.
    - Optionally, decorate with maraschino cherries on top.

5. **Chill and serve:**
    - Refrigerate the cake for at least 1 hour before serving to allow the flavors to meld.
    - Slice and serve chilled. Enjoy the rich, chocolatey, and cherry-filled layers of this classic Black Forest Cake!

Tips:

- For best results, use high-quality cocoa powder for a rich chocolate flavor in the cake.
- Make sure the heavy cream is well chilled before whipping to achieve stiff peaks.
- Store leftover cake covered in the refrigerator. It can be stored for up to 3 days.

This Black Forest Cake recipe is perfect for celebrations and special occasions, combining moist chocolate cake layers with cherries and whipped cream for a delightful and indulgent dessert experience.

Panna Cotta

Ingredients:

- 2 cups heavy cream
- 1/2 cup whole milk
- 1/2 cup granulated sugar
- 1 vanilla bean, split lengthwise and seeds scraped out (or 1 teaspoon vanilla extract)
- 2 1/4 teaspoons powdered gelatin (about 1 packet)
- 3 tablespoons cold water

Instructions:

1. **Prepare the gelatin:**
    - In a small bowl, sprinkle the gelatin over the cold water. Let it sit for about 5-10 minutes to bloom and soften.
2. **Heat the cream mixture:**
    - In a saucepan, combine the heavy cream, whole milk, sugar, and vanilla bean seeds (or vanilla extract).
    - Heat the mixture over medium heat, stirring occasionally, until it just begins to simmer. Do not boil.
3. **Dissolve the gelatin:**
    - Remove the saucepan from heat. Remove the vanilla bean pod if using.
    - Add the bloomed gelatin to the hot cream mixture. Stir until the gelatin is completely dissolved.
4. **Cool and pour:**
    - Allow the mixture to cool slightly for about 10-15 minutes, stirring occasionally.
    - Strain the mixture through a fine-mesh sieve into a pouring jug to remove any clumps or vanilla bean remnants.
5. **Pour into molds or serving dishes:**
    - Pour the panna cotta mixture into individual ramekins, molds, or serving glasses.
    - Fill each mold to about 3/4 full.
6. **Chill and set:**
    - Refrigerate the panna cotta for at least 4 hours, or until set. It should be firm to the touch.
7. **Serve:**
    - To unmold, run a knife around the edge of each panna cotta and carefully invert onto serving plates. If serving in glasses or ramekins, serve as is.
    - Optionally, garnish with fresh berries, fruit coulis, caramel sauce, or a sprinkle of powdered cocoa before serving.
8. **Enjoy:**
    - Serve chilled and enjoy the creamy, velvety texture of vanilla panna cotta.

Tips:

- For a lighter version, you can use half-and-half or even substitute part of the cream with Greek yogurt.
- Experiment with different flavors by infusing the cream mixture with other ingredients such as citrus zest, coffee, or spices like cinnamon.
- Panna cotta can be made a day ahead and stored in the refrigerator, covered, until ready to serve.

This vanilla panna cotta recipe is elegant yet simple, making it a perfect dessert for both casual dinners and formal gatherings. Its smooth texture and delicate flavor make it a favorite among dessert enthusiasts.

Caramel Popcorn

Ingredients:

- 12 cups popped popcorn (about 1/2 cup unpopped kernels)
- 1 cup unsalted butter
- 2 cups packed light brown sugar
- 1/2 cup light corn syrup
- 1 teaspoon salt
- 1/2 teaspoon baking soda
- 1 teaspoon vanilla extract

Instructions:

1. **Preheat and prepare:**
   - Preheat your oven to 250°F (120°C). Line a large baking sheet with parchment paper or a silicone baking mat. Lightly grease the parchment paper or mat with cooking spray or butter.
2. **Pop the popcorn:**
   - Pop the popcorn kernels using an air popper or stove-top method. Make sure to remove any unpopped kernels. Transfer the popped popcorn to a large mixing bowl. You may need to do this in batches.
3. **Make the caramel sauce:**
   - In a medium saucepan, melt the butter over medium heat.
   - Stir in the brown sugar, corn syrup, and salt. Cook, stirring constantly, until the mixture comes to a boil.
4. **Cook the caramel:**
   - Once boiling, continue to cook without stirring for 4-5 minutes. The mixture should reach a temperature of about 250°F (120°C) on a candy thermometer, or until it reaches the soft ball stage (a small amount dropped into cold water forms a soft ball).
5. **Add baking soda and vanilla:**
   - Remove the saucepan from heat and carefully stir in the baking soda and vanilla extract. The mixture will bubble up, so be cautious.
6. **Coat the popcorn:**
   - Immediately pour the caramel sauce over the popped popcorn in the mixing bowl.
   - Use a spatula or wooden spoon to gently toss and coat the popcorn evenly with the caramel sauce.
7. **Bake the caramel popcorn:**
   - Spread the coated popcorn evenly onto the prepared baking sheet.
   - Bake in the preheated oven for 45-60 minutes, stirring every 15 minutes to ensure even coating and prevent burning.
8. **Cool and break apart:**
   - Remove the baking sheet from the oven and let the caramel popcorn cool completely on the baking sheet.

- Once cooled, break the caramel popcorn into clusters or individual pieces.
9. **Serve and store:**
    - Transfer the caramel popcorn to an airtight container or serve immediately for a crunchy and sweet snack.
    - Store any leftovers in an airtight container at room temperature for up to one week.

Tips:

- For a variation, you can add nuts (such as peanuts or almonds) or drizzle melted chocolate over the cooled caramel popcorn before it fully sets.
- Be careful when working with hot caramel as it can cause burns. Use caution and supervise closely if making this recipe with children.
- Customize the sweetness and saltiness to your preference by adjusting the amount of brown sugar and salt used.

Homemade caramel popcorn is perfect for movie nights, parties, or as a special homemade gift. Its crunchy texture and sweet caramel flavor make it a favorite treat for both kids and adults alike!

White Chocolate Blondies

Ingredients:

- 1 cup unsalted butter, melted
- 1 cup light brown sugar, packed
- 1/2 cup granulated sugar
- 2 large eggs
- 1 tablespoon vanilla extract
- 2 cups all-purpose flour
- 1/2 teaspoon baking powder
- 1/2 teaspoon salt
- 1 cup white chocolate chips or chopped white chocolate

Instructions:

1. **Preheat** your oven to 350°F (175°C). Grease or line a 9x13-inch baking pan with parchment paper.
2. **Mix the wet ingredients:**
   - In a large mixing bowl, whisk together the melted butter, light brown sugar, and granulated sugar until well combined.
3. **Add eggs and vanilla:**
   - Add the eggs one at a time, mixing well after each addition.
   - Stir in the vanilla extract until incorporated.
4. **Combine dry ingredients:**
   - In a separate bowl, whisk together the flour, baking powder, and salt.
5. **Mix wet and dry ingredients:**
   - Gradually add the dry ingredients to the wet ingredients, mixing until just combined. Do not overmix.
6. **Add white chocolate:**
   - Fold in the white chocolate chips or chopped white chocolate until evenly distributed throughout the batter.
7. **Bake the blondies:**
   - Spread the batter evenly into the prepared baking pan, smoothing the top with a spatula.
   - Bake in the preheated oven for 25-30 minutes, or until the top is golden brown and a toothpick inserted into the center comes out with moist crumbs (not wet batter).
8. **Cool and slice:**
   - Remove the blondies from the oven and let them cool completely in the pan on a wire rack.
   - Once cooled, lift the blondies out of the pan using the parchment paper and transfer to a cutting board.
   - Cut into squares or rectangles of desired size.
9. **Serve and enjoy:**
   - Serve the white chocolate blondies at room temperature or slightly warmed, if desired.

- Store leftovers in an airtight container at room temperature for up to 3 days, or in the refrigerator for longer freshness.

Tips:

- For an extra indulgent treat, drizzle melted white chocolate over the cooled blondies before serving.
- You can add chopped nuts (such as macadamia nuts or pecans) for added texture and flavor.
- Make sure not to overbake the blondies to keep them soft and chewy.

These white chocolate blondies are perfect for satisfying your sweet tooth with their rich, buttery flavor and creamy white chocolate chunks. Enjoy them as a dessert or a special treat any time of day!

Lavender Shortbread

Ingredients:

- 1 cup unsalted butter, softened
- 1/2 cup granulated sugar
- 2 cups all-purpose flour
- 1 tablespoon culinary lavender buds (dried and food-grade)
- 1/4 teaspoon salt
- Optional: Additional granulated sugar or powdered sugar for dusting

Instructions:

1. **Preheat your oven** to 325°F (160°C). Line a baking sheet with parchment paper or silicone baking mat.
2. **Prepare the lavender:** Grind the culinary lavender buds using a mortar and pestle or a spice grinder until finely ground. You want the lavender to be fine enough to incorporate evenly into the dough.
3. **Cream the butter and sugar:** In a large mixing bowl, beat together the softened butter and granulated sugar until light and fluffy.
4. **Add the lavender and salt:** Add the ground lavender and salt to the butter mixture. Mix until well combined.
5. **Incorporate the flour:** Gradually add the flour to the butter mixture, mixing until a dough forms. Use your hands to bring the dough together if needed.
6. **Shape the dough:** Transfer the dough onto a lightly floured surface. Shape the dough into a ball and flatten it into a disk about 1/2 inch (1.3 cm) thick.
7. **Cut the shortbread:** Using a cookie cutter or a sharp knife, cut the dough into desired shapes (rounds, squares, rectangles, etc.). Re-roll any scraps and cut out more shapes until all the dough is used.
8. **Chill (optional):** Place the cut-out shortbread cookies on the prepared baking sheet. If time allows, chill the cookies in the refrigerator for 15-30 minutes. Chilling helps the cookies retain their shape during baking.
9. **Bake the shortbread:** Bake in the preheated oven for 15-18 minutes, or until the edges are lightly golden brown.
10. **Cool and serve:** Remove from the oven and let the shortbread cool on the baking sheet for 5 minutes. Then transfer to a wire rack to cool completely.
11. **Optional: Dust with sugar:** Once cooled, you can dust the tops of the lavender shortbread with a sprinkle of granulated sugar or powdered sugar for an extra touch.
12. **Store:** Store the cooled lavender shortbread cookies in an airtight container at room temperature. They will keep well for up to one week.

Tips:

- Ensure your lavender is culinary grade and suitable for consumption.
- Adjust the amount of lavender to your preference. If you prefer a stronger lavender flavor, you can add a bit more, but be cautious as too much can overwhelm the taste.

- Serve these lavender shortbread cookies with tea or coffee for a delightful treat, or package them as a lovely homemade gift.

Enjoy the delicate floral aroma and buttery richness of these lavender shortbread cookies!

Churros

Ingredients:

- 1 cup water
- 1/2 cup unsalted butter
- 1/4 teaspoon salt
- 1 cup all-purpose flour
- 3 large eggs
- Vegetable oil, for frying
- 1/2 cup granulated sugar
- 1 teaspoon ground cinnamon

Instructions:

1. **Prepare the churro dough:**
   - In a medium saucepan, combine water, butter, and salt. Bring to a boil over medium heat.
2. **Add flour:**
   - Remove from heat and quickly stir in the flour until it forms a ball of dough. This should happen very quickly.
3. **Mix in eggs:**
   - Transfer the dough to a mixing bowl. Add the eggs one at a time, mixing well after each addition. The dough should be smooth and glossy.
4. **Heat oil for frying:**
   - In a deep skillet or pot, heat about 2 inches of vegetable oil to 350°F (175°C).
5. **Pipe the churros:**
   - Transfer the churro dough to a pastry bag fitted with a large star tip (such as Wilton 1M). Pipe 4-6 inch strips of dough directly into the hot oil, using scissors to cut the dough from the pastry bag.
6. **Fry until golden brown:**
   - Fry the churros for 2-3 minutes per side, or until they are golden brown and crispy. Fry in batches to avoid overcrowding the pan.
7. **Drain and coat:**
   - Remove the fried churros with a slotted spoon or tongs and drain on a plate lined with paper towels to absorb excess oil.
8. **Coat with cinnamon sugar:**
   - In a shallow dish, combine the granulated sugar and ground cinnamon. Roll the warm churros in the cinnamon sugar mixture until evenly coated.
9. **Serve and enjoy:**
   - Serve the churros warm, optionally with chocolate sauce, caramel sauce, or dulce de leche for dipping.

Tips:

- The key to crispy churros is ensuring that the oil is hot enough before frying.

- If you don't have a pastry bag, you can use a sturdy plastic storage bag with a corner cut off.
- For a twist, you can fill the churros with chocolate ganache or dulce de leche using a piping bag fitted with a small round tip.

Homemade churros are a delightful treat, perfect for enjoying as a dessert or special snack. Their crispy exterior and soft, doughy interior make them a favorite in many households and at celebrations!

Peppermint Bark

Ingredients:

- 12 ounces (about 2 cups) high-quality dark chocolate, chopped or chocolate chips
- 12 ounces (about 2 cups) high-quality white chocolate, chopped or white chocolate chips
- 1/2 teaspoon peppermint extract, divided
- 1/2 cup crushed candy canes or peppermint candies, divided

Instructions:

1. **Prepare a baking sheet:**
   - Line a baking sheet with parchment paper or a silicone baking mat.
2. **Melt the dark chocolate:**
   - In a heatproof bowl set over a pot of simmering water (double boiler method), melt the dark chocolate, stirring occasionally until smooth.
   - Alternatively, melt the dark chocolate in the microwave in 30-second intervals, stirring well after each interval until melted and smooth.
3. **Add peppermint extract:**
   - Stir in 1/4 teaspoon of peppermint extract into the melted dark chocolate until well combined.
4. **Spread dark chocolate:**
   - Pour the melted dark chocolate onto the prepared baking sheet. Use an offset spatula or the back of a spoon to spread it into an even layer about 1/4-inch thick.
5. **Chill dark chocolate layer:**
   - Place the baking sheet in the refrigerator for about 15-20 minutes, or until the dark chocolate layer is firm.
6. **Melt the white chocolate:**
   - In another heatproof bowl, melt the white chocolate using the same method as the dark chocolate (double boiler or microwave).
7. **Add peppermint extract and candy canes:**
   - Stir in the remaining 1/4 teaspoon of peppermint extract into the melted white chocolate until well combined.
   - Mix in about 1/4 cup of the crushed candy canes or peppermint candies, reserving the rest for topping.
8. **Spread white chocolate layer:**
   - Remove the baking sheet from the refrigerator. Pour the melted white chocolate over the chilled dark chocolate layer.
   - Use a spatula to spread the white chocolate evenly over the dark chocolate layer.
9. **Sprinkle with toppings:**
   - Immediately sprinkle the remaining crushed candy canes or peppermint candies evenly over the melted white chocolate layer, pressing them lightly into the chocolate.
10. **Chill to set:**
    - Return the baking sheet to the refrigerator and chill for about 30 minutes to 1 hour, or until the peppermint bark is completely set and firm.
11. **Break into pieces:**

- Once set, remove the peppermint bark from the baking sheet and break it into pieces using your hands or a knife.
12. **Serve or store:**
    - Serve the peppermint bark immediately, or store it in an airtight container in the refrigerator until ready to serve. It can also be wrapped and given as a homemade holiday gift.

Tips:

- Use high-quality chocolate for the best flavor and texture.
- Adjust the amount of peppermint extract to suit your preference for a more or less intense peppermint flavor.
- Store peppermint bark in the refrigerator to keep it firm, especially in warmer climates.

Peppermint bark is a delicious treat that combines the richness of chocolate with the refreshing taste of peppermint, making it a perfect homemade holiday treat or gift idea.

Apple Crisp

Ingredients:

For the filling:

- 6 cups peeled, cored, and sliced apples (about 5-6 medium apples, such as Granny Smith or Honeycrisp)
- 1/4 cup granulated sugar
- 1 tablespoon all-purpose flour
- 1 teaspoon ground cinnamon
- 1/4 teaspoon ground nutmeg (optional)
- 1 tablespoon lemon juice

For the topping:

- 3/4 cup old-fashioned rolled oats
- 1/2 cup all-purpose flour
- 1/2 cup packed light brown sugar
- 1/4 teaspoon salt
- 1/2 cup unsalted butter, cold and cut into small pieces

Instructions:

1. **Preheat your oven** to 350°F (175°C). Grease a 9x9-inch baking dish or a similar size baking dish.
2. **Prepare the apple filling:**
   - In a large bowl, combine the sliced apples, granulated sugar, flour, cinnamon, nutmeg (if using), and lemon juice. Toss until the apples are evenly coated.
3. **Transfer to baking dish:**
   - Spread the apple mixture evenly into the prepared baking dish.
4. **Make the topping:**
   - In a separate bowl, combine the rolled oats, flour, brown sugar, and salt.
   - Cut in the cold butter using a pastry cutter or your fingers until the mixture resembles coarse crumbs and the butter is well incorporated.
5. **Assemble and bake:**
   - Sprinkle the oat topping evenly over the apples in the baking dish.
6. **Bake the apple crisp:**
   - Bake in the preheated oven for 40-45 minutes, or until the topping is golden brown and the apples are tender and bubbly.
7. **Cool and serve:**
   - Remove from the oven and let the apple crisp cool for a few minutes before serving.
8. **Serve warm:**
   - Serve the apple crisp warm, optionally with vanilla ice cream or whipped cream.

Tips:

- You can adjust the sweetness of the apple filling according to your taste and the tartness of the apples used.
- Feel free to add chopped nuts (such as pecans or walnuts) to the topping for extra crunch and flavor.
- Store any leftovers covered in the refrigerator. Reheat individual portions in the microwave or oven before serving.

Apple crisp is a delicious and cozy dessert, perfect for fall and winter seasons when apples are in abundance. Enjoy the combination of soft, baked apples with the crunchy oat topping for a delightful treat!

Chocolate Covered Strawberries

Ingredients:

- Fresh strawberries (about 1 pound or 450 grams), washed and dried thoroughly
- 8 ounces (225 grams) high-quality semi-sweet or dark chocolate, chopped (or chocolate chips)
- Optional: White chocolate, melted (for drizzling)

Instructions:

1. **Prepare the strawberries:**
    - Wash the strawberries under cold water and pat them dry completely with paper towels. It's important for the strawberries to be dry to ensure the chocolate adheres well.
2. **Melt the chocolate:**
    - Place the chopped semi-sweet or dark chocolate in a heatproof bowl. You can melt the chocolate using one of the following methods:
        - **Double boiler method:** Fill a small saucepan with an inch of water and bring it to a simmer. Place the bowl with chocolate on top, making sure the bottom of the bowl does not touch the water. Stir the chocolate occasionally until melted and smooth.
        - **Microwave method:** Microwave the chocolate in 30-second intervals, stirring well after each interval, until melted and smooth. Be careful not to overheat the chocolate.
3. **Dip the strawberries:**
    - Hold each strawberry by the stem and dip it into the melted chocolate, swirling to coat it evenly. Allow any excess chocolate to drip back into the bowl.
4. **Place on a baking sheet:**
    - Line a baking sheet with parchment paper or wax paper. Place each chocolate-coated strawberry onto the prepared baking sheet, spacing them slightly apart.
5. **Optional: Drizzle with white chocolate (decorative):**
    - Melt the white chocolate using the same method as the dark chocolate. Transfer the melted white chocolate to a small piping bag or a zip-top bag with a small corner snipped off. Drizzle the white chocolate over the dipped strawberries in a zigzag pattern.
6. **Chill to set:**
    - Place the baking sheet with the chocolate covered strawberries in the refrigerator for about 30 minutes to 1 hour, or until the chocolate is set.
7. **Serve and enjoy:**
    - Once the chocolate has hardened, transfer the chocolate covered strawberries to a serving plate or enjoy them directly from the baking sheet.

Tips:

- Use ripe, but firm strawberries for best results. Avoid strawberries that are overly ripe or soft as they may not hold up well during dipping.
- Experiment with different types of chocolate coatings, such as milk chocolate or white chocolate, or add toppings like chopped nuts, sprinkles, or shredded coconut before the chocolate sets.
- Store chocolate covered strawberries in the refrigerator, but bring them to room temperature for about 15-20 minutes before serving for the best taste and texture.

Chocolate covered strawberries are a simple yet elegant dessert that combines the natural sweetness of strawberries with the richness of chocolate. They make a stunning addition to any dessert table or a thoughtful gift for someone special.

Lemon Meringue Pie

Ingredients:

For the crust:

- 1 1/4 cups all-purpose flour
- 1/2 teaspoon salt
- 1/2 cup unsalted butter, chilled and cut into small pieces
- 3-4 tablespoons ice water

For the lemon filling:

- 1 cup granulated sugar
- 1/4 cup cornstarch
- 1/4 teaspoon salt
- 1 1/2 cups water
- 4 large egg yolks, lightly beaten
- 1 tablespoon lemon zest (from about 2 lemons)
- 1/2 cup freshly squeezed lemon juice (from about 3-4 lemons)
- 2 tablespoons unsalted butter

For the meringue:

- 4 large egg whites, at room temperature
- 1/4 teaspoon cream of tartar
- 1/2 cup granulated sugar

Instructions:

1. Make the crust:

- In a food processor, combine the flour and salt. Add the chilled butter and pulse until the mixture resembles coarse crumbs.
- Gradually add the ice water, 1 tablespoon at a time, pulsing until the dough starts to come together.
- Transfer the dough to a lightly floured surface and knead briefly until smooth. Shape into a disk, wrap in plastic wrap, and refrigerate for at least 30 minutes.

2. Preheat your oven:

- Preheat oven to 375°F (190°C). Roll out the chilled dough on a lightly floured surface to fit a 9-inch pie dish. Transfer the dough to the pie dish, trim any excess, and crimp the edges decoratively. Prick the bottom of the crust with a fork.

3. Blind bake the crust:

- Line the pie crust with parchment paper or foil and fill with pie weights or dried beans. Bake for 15 minutes. Remove the parchment and weights, and bake for an additional 10-12 minutes, or until the crust is golden brown. Remove from the oven and set aside to cool.

4. Make the lemon filling:

- In a medium saucepan, whisk together the sugar, cornstarch, and salt. Gradually whisk in the water until smooth.
- Cook over medium heat, stirring constantly, until the mixture thickens and comes to a boil (about 5-7 minutes).
- Remove from heat. Gradually whisk about 1/2 cup of the hot sugar mixture into the beaten egg yolks to temper them, then whisk the egg mixture back into the saucepan.
- Return to heat and cook, stirring constantly, until the mixture thickens again (about 2 minutes).
- Remove from heat and stir in the lemon zest, lemon juice, and butter until smooth. Pour the filling into the cooled pie crust.

5. Make the meringue:

- In a clean, dry mixing bowl, beat the egg whites and cream of tartar with an electric mixer on medium speed until soft peaks form.
- Gradually add the granulated sugar, 1 tablespoon at a time, beating on high speed until stiff, glossy peaks form and all the sugar is dissolved.

6. Assemble and bake the pie:

- Spread the meringue evenly over the hot lemon filling, making sure to spread it all the way to the edges of the crust to seal.
- Use the back of a spoon to create decorative peaks in the meringue.
- Bake in the preheated oven for 10-12 minutes, or until the meringue is lightly golden brown.

7. Cool and serve:

- Remove from the oven and cool the pie on a wire rack for 1 hour.
- Refrigerate for at least 3 hours, or until the pie is completely chilled and set.
- Slice and serve chilled. Enjoy the tangy lemon filling and fluffy meringue topping!

Tips:

- For best results, use fresh lemon juice and zest for the filling.
- Be careful when tempering the egg yolks to avoid scrambling them.
- Store leftover lemon meringue pie covered in the refrigerator for up to 3 days.

This lemon meringue pie recipe combines the perfect balance of sweet and tart flavors, making it a timeless dessert that's sure to impress!

www.ingramcontent.com/pod-product-compliance
Lightning Source LLC
LaVergne TN
LVHW061945070526
838199LV00060B/3976